cooking easier, healthier & better

75+ DELICIOUS RECIPES

RULE THE KITCHEN®

3-in-1

COOKING SYSTEM

Although every precaution has been taken in the preparation of this book, the publisher and authors assume no responsibility for errors or omissions. Nor is there any liability assumed for damages resulting from the use of the information contained herein. Although every effort has been made to ensure that the information contained in this book is complete and accurate, neither the publisher nor the authors are engaged in rendering professional advice or services to the individual reader. This information is not intended to replace the advice of a medical practitioner and consumers should always consult with a health care professional prior to making changes to diet or lifestyle, including any new health-related eating programs. Neither the publisher nor the authors shall be held responsible for any loss or damage allegedly arising from any information or suggestion in this book. The opinions expressed in this book represent the personal views of the authors and not that of the publisher.

Nutritional Analyses: Calculations for the nutritional analyses in this book are based on the largest number of servings listed within the recipes. Calculations are rounded up to the nearest gram or milligram, as appropriate. If two options for an ingredient are listed, the first one is used. Not included are optional ingredients or serving suggestions.

Editors: Mona Wetter Dolgov and Ronda DiGuglielmo • Graphic Designer: Leslie Anne Feagley
Photo Creative Director: Anne Sommers Welch • Photography: Quentin Bacon • Additional Photography: Gary Sloan and Heath Robbins • Food Stylist: Mariana Velasquez • Recipe Development: Euro-Pro Test Kitchen Team and Culinary Palette, Amy Golino, Kimberly Letizia, and Vanessa Spilios

Published in the United States of America by
Great Chefs International
New Hope, PA 18938
www.greatchefsinternational.com

ISBN-13: 978-4-934193-80-8
Printed in China

TABLE OF CONTENTS

YOUR NINJA COOKING SYSTEM
COOKING EASIER, EATING BETTER

One thing almost everybody has in common today: there are tons of things to manage and the clock is always ticking. Wherever we go, whatever we do, it seems like we never have enough time to do the things we want to do. Whether you are a seasoned home chef or a novice in the kitchen trying to get a quick meal on the table, your Ninja 3-in-1 Cooking System will help you make your meals more flavorful and healthier, with ease, speed, and true convenience.

The Ninja 3-in-1 Cooking System with Triple Fusion Heat Technology does it all. This revolutionary advanced system combines oven, stovetop cooking, slow cooking, steam roasting, and baking technology to enhance flavors, making meats juicier, meals healthier, and desserts more moist, and elevating your family meals from ordinary to extraordinary. It puts success on your table with these versatile features:

FAST ONE-POT MEAL MAKING — Now, with your Ninja Cooking System's Triple Fusion Heat Technology, you can make complete meals for your family in just one single pot. You can layer meals and cook pasta, veggies, and meats all at the same time — pasta does not even have to be drained! Casseroles come out extra crispy on both the bottom and sides. You can even prepare delicious meals from frozen and take them right to your table in 30 minutes or less. Use either the STOVETOP or Triple Fusion Heat oven setting!

STEAM OVEN ROASTING — How to bring out the best quality in practically any cut of meat? Sear first by using STOVETOP HIGH, place meat on roasting rack, and then simply add water to the pot to create a steam infusion. Set to your desired temperature, and begin steam roasting! Steam-infused roasting cuts the cooking time by up to 30% and makes your meats juicier. By adding fresh or dried herbs, broth, or wine to your water, you'll add extra-delicious flavors. Try some of our recommended flavor infusions in our chart provided for added inspiration.

STEAM OVEN BAKING — Baking this fresh way might be new to you. But it's one more feature that makes the Ninja 3-in-1 Cooking System a true breakthrough appliance. Leave your kitchen oven off. You'll find that steam baking delivers lighter, richer puddings and moist, higher-rising cakes. Plus, you only have to use half the fat! This means healthier, lower-calorie desserts — even less than 50 calories — using this new revolutionary style to bake!

SEARIOUS/SLOW COOKING — To make more flavorful meals, professional chefs sear meats and sauté vegetables before slow cooking. Until now, that meant an extra step of heating up a second skillet pan, and at least one more pan to wash. The Ninja 3-in-1 Cooking System lets you sear, brown, and slow cook meats right in the same appliance, with its built-in stovetop. Plus, the slow cooker is programmable, allowing you to set the cooking time, and it will automatically keep warm once cooking is complete. It's a convenient way to cook, making meal preparation and cleanup easier.

USING THE NINJA COOKING SYSTEM COOKBOOK

This cookbook provides recipes and tips you'll find invaluable. They'll help you use the Ninja 3-in-1 Cooking System to simplify your preparation for all of your meals.

Take a minute to look them over. We've included 75 recipes, each customized for the Ninja 3-in-1 Cooking System, that have all been developed and tested in our Ninja kitchens. The recipes tell you exactly what you need for the dish and how to prepare it — clear directions for reliable success. At the top of each recipe, we explain benefits and best uses. You'll also find at least one tip for healthy ingredient choices, time-saving methods, or serving suggestions.

Eight chapters share the secrets of using the Ninja 3-in-1 Cooking System for exciting results:

30-MINUTE MEALS: Easy meals perfect for a weeknight — fast, satisfying, complete.

LITE FARE (HEALTHY & DELICIOUS): Healthier meals, with an eye on lower calories and fat.

APPETIZERS: Formal starters or yummy party snacks for entertaining.

SOUPS/STEWS: Hearty and savory, even perfect for a lighter meal!

ENTREES: Main courses your family — and even guests — will love.

SIDE DISHES: Speedy, delicious accompaniments all made in one pot!

DESSERTS: Tempting treats made healthier without the need of your home stove.

BREAKFASTS: Surprise! Make the first meal of the day easy and delicious!

Time to get started! Pick a recipe from any chapter and give it a try. We built the Ninja 3-in-1 Cooking System to make your life easier. It's one kitchen appliance that eliminates problems and guesswork. Use it every day to save time while preparing meals you're proud to serve.

Have fun!
The NINJA Kitchen Team

 **Stovetop**

SEAR & SAUTÉ — It's a trick that savvy cooks have known for years — searing and browning meat and sautéing vegetables develops added flavors, color, and texture to your meals. The result: tender, juicier, more flavorful meats, and sweeter, aromatic vegetables. Searing meats especially adds attractive color, crusty texture, and flavor contrast you expect from the best restaurant meals. You can now bring that same quality to your home-cooked meals simply and easily, all in one pot.

For the first time, the Ninja 3-in-1 Cooking System lets you sear, brown, or sauté using the STOVETOP setting. It's quick and simple. Just put the ingredients in the pot, set the STOVETOP to the correct setting, and go!

Tips & Tricks

1. **The preset temperatures are similar to your stovetop on LOW, MED, or HIGH.**

2. **Do not use the lid when using the STOVETOP HIGH SETTING TO PREVENT BURNING OF FOOD.**

3. **Use the STOVETOP MED-HIGH setting to make gravies from your liquids after you roast — all in the same pot!**

4. **For healthier cooking, remove any excess fat from the cooking pot before roasting. Be sure to wear protective mitts when handling the unit.**

5. **For quicker browning, set to STOVETOP HIGH for 2 to 3 minutes before placing ingredients in pot.**

This STOVETOP feature is versatile, too. The LOW setting simmers soups and sauces, MED perfectly sautés aromatics like onions and garlic, and browns meats and tender vegetables, and HIGH sears meats just right. Also use the MED and HIGH settings to prepare a complete skillet or stir-fry dinner, and to reheat dinners, too!

Use the STOVETOP setting for sequential cooking — that means, sear meats on STOVETOP HIGH before you slow cook or steam roast to prepare the most delicious meals. This setting will allow your ingredients to lock in the flavor!

Fast One-Pot Meal Making

ONE-POT MEALS — Your Ninja 3-in-1 Cooking System's Triple Fusion Heat Technology provides heat to both the sides and bottom of the pot that allows you to create complete meals all at the same time — from Quick Shrimp Scampi to Spaghetti & Meatballs! This means no extra pans for browning foods or preparing more complex dishes. Now, when your meals are complete, you will have only one pot to clean. You can even prepare meals with pasta in the same pot — by layering the foods in the right way, pasta will be ready, without the need to drain!

LAYERED MEALS — For the first time, you can prepare complete meals in a single pot. Even challenging dishes like layered casseroles cook up beautifully with every ingredient done properly — vegetables, crispy toppings, and meats prepared to family-pleasing perfection. The roasting rack included can accommodate the different meal components. Typically, place your starch on the bottom with the appropriate broth or water, and place your protein and vegetables on the roasting rack during cooking. The rack makes it easy to check for doneness and to remove each meal component when it is perfectly cooked.

Achieve impressive food quality with one-pot convenience!

Tips & Tricks

1. Dense root vegetables cook slower than many meat cuts or more tender veggies. Cut them into small uniform pieces so they'll cook at the same rate as other ingredients.

2. Vegetables can be added with starches in layered meals to create more flavorful dishes.

3. Frozen fish and chicken breasts cook perfectly on the roasting rack or right in the pot, and you can prepare meals in less than 30 minutes.

4. See our charts in the back of the book for cooking guides for meats, vegetables, and starches for inspiration and to manage getting your meals complete at the same time.

CAVATELLI & BROCOLLI ALFREDO • PAGE 27

 SEARious Slow Cooking

SLOW COOKING — The Ninja 3-in-1 Cooking System is also a SEARious slow cooker — the STOVETOP setting allows you to sear your meats first, then SLOW COOK all in the same appliance! Searing not only gives great texture, it also builds flavor profiles that will elevate your dishes to gourmet quality. The SLOW COOK feature allows you to cook food all day, and it is safe to leave home while cooking! Cook on LOW for all-day cooking, or cook on HIGH in half the time, great for weekend comfort-food cooking. Whether cooking savory Hearty Beef Stew, Pulled Pork & Apple Cider Sliders, or White Turkey Chili, this portable countertop appliance offers versatile convenience when cooking new and old favorite recipes to treat your family and friends all year long. In addition, use your SEARious slow cooker to make healthier and lighter vegetable dishes, too! See all of our delicious recipes!

Tips & Tricks

1. **Never fill your pot more than 2/3 full to ensure food is cooked appropriately.**

2. **Lifting the lid during cooking may increase the total cook time.**

3. **Because our slow cooking uses very little energy, it is great to slow cook in the hot summer months to keep your kitchen cool.**

4. **While some frozen foods can be cooked successfully in the slow-cooker mode, it may increase the total cook time. Always use an instant-read thermometer to ensure that foods are cooked to the correct internal temperature. Large frozen roasts are not recommended to be slow cooked. To ensure proper cook time and doneness, it is best to thaw meat safely in the refrigerator before cooking.**

5. **Certain dried spices can even intensify during slow cooking such as chili pepper powders, cayenne, and red pepper flakes. Use half of the amount of hot spice at the beginning, and add more at the end if necessary.**

6. **Pouring off or skimming fat that has rendered off during searing or slow cooking will reduce the overall fat content of your dishes to make them healthier for your family.**

7. **Use the programmability — set the cooking time, and the unit will automatically shift to KEEP WARM until you are ready to enjoy!**

WHITE TURKEY CHILI • PAGE 58

Steam Oven

STEAM ROASTING — The Ninja 3-in-1 Cooking System has steam-oven capability to make your meats juicier and cut cooking time by up to 30%! The combination of radiant and steam heat makes preparation of poultry, beef, pork, and even fish simple, easy, and delicious. Taking less time and cooking in a steam environment results in juicy, flavorful roasts. You will taste the difference right away… tender, flavorful perfection.

It's easy to steam roast! Simply add water or flavorful infusion into the pot. Place the roasting rack with your seasoned meat into the pot, set the oven to your desired temperature setting, set the cook time, and start roasting. You will not only save cooking time, but there is also NO PREHEATING REQUIRED!

We've described a series of flavor infusions that actually bring rich taste into the food while it cooks. Check out our flavor-infusion charts in the back of the book for delicious ideas!

Tips & Tricks

1. **Spray the roasting rack with nonstick cooking spray before you cook. Meats won't stick and cleanup will be even easier.**

2. **Arranging foods in even layers on the rack promotes even cooking.**

3. **Wait 5 to 10 minutes after roasting meat before you serve, to let the meat rest and the juices settle. The juices distribute evenly, and everything tastes even better.**

4. **Keep the rack level when you lift it out so food won't slide or roll off.**

5. **Protect yourself — always use oven mitts or pot holders when you remove the roasting rack.**

6. **Try roasting with or without the rack. Many cooks make a "rack" of root or aromatic vegetables (like shallots, onion chunks, or potatoes) to support the meat. This adds flavor in both directions.**

SWEET & SPICY PORK BABY BACK RIBS • PAGE 74

🍳 Steam Baking

STEAM BAKING — The Ninja 3-in-1 Cooking System also steam bakes to make your desserts moister and healthier. By baking in a steam environment, you only have to use HALF the fat, plus you get cakes that are spongier and more delicious. This results in healthier desserts that taste delicious! Prepare tasty cupcakes and loaf cakes — cheesecakes and pudding cakes also taste lighter and more delicious! It's an easy way to indulge, and save calories!

It is really simple to steam bake in the Ninja 3-in-1 Cooking System. Place water at the bottom of the pot. Place your baking pan with batter on the roasting rack, set to OVEN, set your desired temperature and time, and start baking!

Tips & Tricks

1. **The pot's nonstick coating makes a great baking surface. You'll only need a nonstick spray if the recipe calls for it.**

2. **Always use oven mitts or pot holders when you remove the roasting rack from the pot.**

3. **A handy rule of thumb for steam baking: Add a cup of water for about every 10 minutes of baking time.**

4. **Fruited topping cakes are made best when the fruit is placed on the bottom of the pan. Lift the cake out of the pan to create delicious fruited upside-down cakes.**

GLUTEN-FREE CHOCOLATE ALMOND MINI CUPCAKES • PAGE 102

COD WITH TOMATO CAPER SAUCE & SUGAR SNAP PEAS • PAGE 26

CHAPTER 1: 30-Minute Meals

 **OVEN**

EASY SPAGHETTI & MEATBALLS

The perfect combination of ingredients means that pasta, meatballs, and sauce can cook together in the pot — no prep needed! This family favorite is a true one-dish meal.

PREP: 5 minutes • **COOK:** 25 minutes • **SERVINGS:** 4

Ingredients

4 cups water

1 pound spaghetti, broken in half

1 jar (24 ounces) pasta sauce (for thinner sauce, reduce water by ¼ cup)

1 package (24 ounces) frozen meatballs

Directions

1. Pour 4 cups water into pot. Stir in spaghetti, sauce, and meatballs. Set OVEN to 300°F for 25 minutes. Cover and cook until pasta is tender and meatballs are hot, stirring occasionally. NOTE: When using thinner sauces, use 3¾ cup water. For whole grain and thicker pastas, increase cooking time by 2–5 minutes, or until pasta is tender. Serve immediately.

NINJA SERVING TIP

Serve with a tossed green salad and garlic bread.

STOVETOP/STEAM OVEN

Signature

CHICKEN PICCATA

Sautéed chicken breasts, quinoa cooked with lemon and wine, and perfectly steamed asparagus, cooked in 30 minutes using only one pot! Layered cooking makes it easy to serve a homemade meal in minutes.

PREP: 5 minutes • **COOK:** 25 minutes • **SERVINGS:** 4

Ingredients

2 tablespoons all-purpose flour

¼ teaspoon salt

⅛ teaspoon ground black pepper

1¼ pounds boneless, skinless, thin-sliced chicken breast halves

2 tablespoons olive oil

2 tablespoons butter

1 cup chicken broth

1 cup dry white wine

⅓ cup lemon juice

¼ cup brined capers, rinsed and drained

1 cup uncooked quinoa, rinsed

1¼ pounds fresh asparagus, cut into ½-inch pieces

Directions

1. Stir flour, salt, and black pepper on plate. Coat chicken with flour mixture.

2. Add oil and butter to pot. Set to STOVETOP HIGH and heat until butter is melted. Add chicken to pot. Cook uncovered 10 minutes or until chicken is lightly browned on both sides. Remove chicken from pot and place on roasting rack.

3. Add broth, wine, lemon juice, and capers to pot. Stir in quinoa. Place rack with chicken in pot, and place asparagus on rack with chicken. Set OVEN to 300°F for 15 minutes. Cover until chicken is cooked through, asparagus is tender, and quinoa breaks apart.

4. Remove asparagus and chicken from pot. Stir quinoa mixture. Turn off pot. Let quinoa mixture stand. Garnish with parsley.

NINJA HEALTHY TIP

Artichokes are a great source of fiber. Stir 1 package (about 9 ounces) frozen artichoke hearts in with the capers in step 3.

STOVETOP/STEAM OVEN

Signature

QUICK SHRIMP SCAMPI

This amazing dish needs almost no prep time! Add uncooked pasta to garlic-wine sauce and stir in frozen shrimp to finish heating at the same time the pasta is cooking.

PREP: 5 minutes • **COOK:** 25 minutes • **SERVINGS:** 4

Ingredients

4 tablespoons butter

4 cloves garlic, minced

¼ teaspoon crushed red pepper

1 cup chopped fresh parsley

Salt and ground black pepper

½ cup dry white wine

4 cups water

1 package (1 pound) angel hair pasta, broken in half

1 pound frozen cooked, peeled, and deveined large shrimp

Directions

1. Place butter into pot. Set to STOVETOP HIGH and heat until butter is melted. Stir in garlic, red pepper, **half** the parsley, salt, and black pepper into pot. Cook uncovered 5 minutes or until garlic is lightly browned, stirring occasionally.

2. Add wine, water, and pasta to pot. Stir to submerge pasta in liquid. Set OVEN to 300°F for 15 minutes. Cover and cook.

3. Add shrimp into pot. Set time for another 10 minutes. Cover and cook until pasta is tender and shrimp are heated through. Sprinkle with remaining parsley.

NINJA TIME-SAVER TIP

Try garlic that is already chopped, sold in jars in the produce department.

STOVETOP

GREEK-STYLE CHICKEN & VEGETABLE PITAS

The filling for these fresh-tasting sandwiches is amazingly quick to make. Chicken is browned for color and flavor, then layered with vegetables to finish cooking simultaneously.

PREP: 5 minutes • **COOK:** 25 minutes • **SERVINGS:** 4

Ingredients

⅓ cup lemon juice

2 tablespoons vegetable or olive oil

1 teaspoon dried oregano leaves, crushed

½ teaspoon ground cumin

1½ pounds skinless, boneless chicken breast halves, cut into cubes

½ pint grape tomatoes

1 yellow squash or green zucchini, cut in half lengthwise, then into 1-inch slices

4 pita breads

Directions

1. Stir lemon juice, oil, oregano, and cumin in bowl. Place chicken and **½ cup** lemon mixture in another bowl and toss to coat. Add tomatoes and squash to remaining lemon mixture and toss to coat.

2. Place chicken into pot. Set to STOVETOP HIGH. Cook uncovered 5 to 10 minutes or until chicken is browned, stirring constantly. Stir zucchini mixture into pot. Cover and cook 10 to 15 minutes or until zucchini is tender and chicken is cooked through.

NINJA TIME-SAVER TIP

Buy cut-up zucchini at the salad bar in your grocery store!

 STOVETOP

STIR-FRIED BEEF & BROCCOLI WITH CELLOPHANE NOODLES

This flavorful stir-fry is quick to make, served over easy-to-make noodles. Cellophane noodles are sometimes called "bean threads" and can be found in the international foods section of most markets.

PREP: 10 minutes • **COOK:** 15 minutes • **SERVINGS:** 4

Ingredients

1 tablespoon vegetable oil

1 pound boneless sirloin beef steak, cut into thin strips

1 clove garlic, minced

1 tablespoon grated fresh ginger

4 cups fresh broccoli florets

¾ cup water

⅛ cup oyster or hoisin sauce

2 tablespoons soy sauce

1 tablespoon rice wine vinegar

1 tablespoon cornstarch

1 package (4 ounces) cellophane noodles, reconstituted according to package directions

Directions

1. Pour oil into pot. Set to STOVETOP HIGH and heat oil. Add beef, garlic, and ginger and cook uncovered 10 minutes or until beef is browned, stirring often. Add broccoli and cook 1 minute.

2. Stir water, oyster sauce, soy sauce, vinegar, and cornstarch in bowl. Add to beef mixture and stir to coat. Cover and cook 3 minutes or until broccoli is tender. Serve beef mixture over noodles.

NINJA SERVING TIP

Serve over rice instead of cellophane noodles for a more traditional twist. For a change of pace, replace broccoli with bell peppers and asparagus or replace beef with chicken strips.

OVEN

COD WITH TOMATO CAPER SAUCE & SUGAR SNAP PEAS

The delicate flavor of cod pairs perfectly with the more assertive flavors of capers, garlic, and basil in the sauce. This flavorful liquid keeps the cod moist and helps cook the sugar snap peas to the perfect tender-crisp texture.

PREP: 5 minutes • **COOK:** 20 minutes • **SERVINGS:** 4

Ingredients

2 medium tomatoes, chopped

½ cup white wine

2 tablespoons drained capers

2 cloves garlic, minced

1 tablespoon chopped fresh basil leaves

½ teaspoon salt

4 cod fillets (about 1 pound)

¾ pound sugar snap peas

Directions

1. Stir tomatoes, wine, capers, garlic, basil, and salt in pot. Add fish to pot. Set OVEN to 375°F for 10 minutes; cover.

2. Place snap peas on fish. Set OVEN to 375°F for 10 minutes. Cover and cook until fish flakes easily when tested with a fork and snap peas are tender-crisp.

 TIME-SAVER TIP

Substitute 1 can (14.5 ounces) diced tomatoes in juice for chopped tomatoes.

 STOVETOP

CAVATELLI & BROCCOLI ALFREDO

This classic Italian dish is made with cavatelli right from the freezer. There's no need to thaw or cook separately — it all cooks right in one pot.

PREP: 5 minutes • **COOK:** 25 minutes • **SERVINGS:** 4

Ingredients

1 tablespoon olive oil

1 small onion, chopped

2 cloves garlic, minced

1 package (about 14 ounces) frozen cavatelli

4 cups broccoli florets

1 jar (15 ounces) light Alfredo sauce

2 cups water

¼ cup shredded Parmesan cheese

Directions

1. Pour oil into pot. Set to STOVETOP HIGH and heat oil. Stir in onion and garlic. Cook uncovered 5 minutes or until onion is tender, stirring occasionally.

2. Stir in cavatelli, broccoli, sauce, and water. Set to STOVETOP MED. Cover and cook 20 minutes or until cavatelli and broccoli are tender. Stir in cheese just before serving.

 SERVING TIP

Frozen tortellini can replace cavatelli, and asparagus and roasted red peppers can replace broccoli for an alternative dish. Adding ¼ cup diced prosciutto also makes a tasty variation.

 STEAM OVEN

SALMON WITH ARUGULA & SUN-DRIED TOMATO COUSCOUS

Substitute any leafy green, such as baby spinach, if arugula is unavailable. Dark green leafy vegetables, such as arugula, are great sources for vitamins A, C, and K; folate; iron; calcium; and fiber.

PREP: 10 minutes • **COOK:** 20 minutes • **SERVINGS:** 4

Ingredients

1½ tablespoons olive oil

1 small onion, chopped

1 cup uncooked couscous

1 cup water

¼ cup sun-dried tomatoes, cut in ¼-inch strips

1 pint grape tomatoes, cut in half

Cooking spray

4 salmon fillets (6 ounces each)

1 package (7 ounces) fresh arugula

Directions

1. Set OVEN to 350°F. Heat oil and stir in onion. Cook uncovered 5 minutes or until onion is tender, stirring occasionally. Stir in couscous, water, sun-dried tomatoes, and grape tomatoes.

2. Spray roasting rack with cooking spray and place into pot. Place fish on rack. Cover and cook 10 to 20 minutes (depending on fish thickness) or until fish flakes easily when tested with fork. Remove fish from pot, cover, and keep warm. Turn off pot.

3. Stir arugula into pot. Serve couscous mixture with fish.

NINJA TIME-SAVER TIP

Look for onions already chopped in the produce section.

 STOVETOP

TOFU, SHIITAKE, & RED PEPPER STIR-FRY

Dusting the tofu with cornstarch gives it a great texture when fried, crispy on the outside and softer in the center.

PREP: 10 minutes • **COOK:** 15 minutes • **SERVINGS:** 4

Ingredients

- 1 package extra-firm tofu, cut into 1- to 2-inch pieces and drained on paper towels
- 5 tablespoons cornstarch, (3 tablespoons for tofu, 2 tablespoons for sauce)
- 3-5 tablespoons canola or vegetable oil, separated
- 2 red peppers, sliced thin
- 1 cup shiitake mushrooms, sliced thin
- 1 bunch of whole scallions, sliced thin on the diagonal, reserving
- 3 cloves of garlic, chopped
- 1 tablespoon fresh ginger, chopped
- ¾ cup vegetable broth
- 3 tablespoons soy sauce
- 1 tablespoon rice wine vinegar
- 2 teaspoons sugar
- Salt and black pepper

Directions

1. In a small bowl, dust the tofu in the cornstarch, covering all sides.

2. On STOVETOP HIGH, heat the oil. Add the tofu and brown on all sides, adding more oil if necessary. Once all of the tofu has been browned (approximately 5 minutes), remove and set aside.

3. Cook the red peppers, shiitake mushrooms, and scallions, stirring frequently until they have softened, about 5 minutes. Set aside. Add a tablespoon of oil and cook the garlic and ginger until fragrant but not browned.

4. Add the ingredients for the sauce and bring to a boil, stirring frequently until the sauce thickens to desired consistency, 5 to 10 minutes. Add the cooked tofu and vegetables to the sauce, stirring to combine. Season to taste with salt and pepper and serve.

NINJA SERVING TIP

This dish can be served with cellophane rice noodles that simply need to be soaked in hot water.

SEA BASS Á LA NAGE WITH STEAMED ROMAINE • PAGE 37

CHAPTER 2:
Lite Fare

STEAM OVEN

Signature

APRICOT & COUNTRY MUSTARD SALMON

The liquid in the bottom of the pot keeps the salmon moist and flavorful. This dish has amazing flavor and it's surprisingly easy to make — with ingredients right from your pantry.

PREP: 5 minutes • **COOK:** 10 minutes • **SERVINGS:** 4

Ingredients

¼ cup apricot preserves

2 tablespoons country
   Dijon-style mustard

2 cups water

1½ pounds salmon fillets

Salt and ground black pepper

Directions

1. Stir preserves and mustard in bowl.

2. Pour 2 cups of water into pot. Season fish with salt and black pepper. Place fish on roasting rack. Spread preserve mixture on fish. Place rack into pot.

3. Set OVEN to 400°F for 20 minutes (for thick fillets), checking after 10 to15 minutes for desired doneness.

NUTRITION PER SERVING: 290 CALORIES; 12G FAT; 2.5G SATURATED FAT; 180MG SODIUM; 13G CARBOHYDRATE; 0G FIBER; 32G PROTEIN

NINJA SERVING TIP

Sprinkle the fish with sliced green onion and serve with baked potatoes and a green salad.

CHICKEN & QUINOA SALAD

Quinoa is an ancient grain high in protein with a nutty flavor. This recipe has three sources of protein but only one pot for cooking!

PREP: 10 minutes • **COOK:** 20 minutes • **SERVINGS:** 4

Ingredients

1 pound skinless, boneless chicken tenderloins

Salt and ground black pepper

2 cups water

1 cup uncooked quinoa, rinsed

¾ cup frozen shelled soybeans, thawed

¾ cup cherry tomatoes, cut in half

⅓ cup chopped walnuts

½ cup chopped parsley

3 tablespoons extra-virgin olive oil

2 tablespoons rice wine vinegar

Directions

1. Season chicken with salt and black pepper.

2. Stir water and quinoa in pot. Set to STOVETOP HIGH. Cover and cook until water heats to a boil.

3. Place chicken on roasting rack and place rack into pot. Set OVEN to 325°F for 15 minutes, checking after 10 minutes. Cover and cook until chicken is cooked through. Remove rack and chicken from pot. Cover chicken to keep warm.

4. Cover pot and cook 5 minutes or until quinoa is tender yet chewy and all water is absorbed. Turn off pot. Stir in soybeans, tomatoes, walnuts, parsley, olive oil, and vinegar. Season with salt and black pepper. Serve with chicken.

NUTRITION PER SERVING: 520 CALORIES; 25G FAT; 3.5G SATURATED FAT; 70MG SODIUM; 34G CARBOHYDRATE; 6G FIBER; 39G PROTEIN

NINJA HEALTHY TIP

Substitute your favorite low-calorie vinaigrette dressing for the oil and vinegar in this recipe. Lima beans and peas can also be substituted for soybeans.

 STOVETOP

CHICKEN, FETA, & SUN-DRIED TOMATO BURGERS

Heat in the pot surrounds chicken patties, seasoned with feta and sun-dried tomatoes, for a well-seared outside and moist flavor sealed inside.

PREP: 10 minutes • **COOK:** 10 minutes • **STAND:** 5 minutes • **SERVINGS:** 4

Ingredients

1 pound ground chicken

⅓ cup crumbled feta cheese

⅓ cup drained chopped sun-dried tomatoes in olive oil; reserve 1 tablespoon oil

5 sprigs fresh oregano, chopped

Salt and ground black pepper

4 multigrain hamburger buns

8 tablespoons low-fat (2%) plain Greek yogurt

1 cup baby arugula leaves

Directions

1. Stir chicken, cheese, tomatoes, and oregano in bowl. Season with salt and black pepper. Shape chicken mixture into 4 burgers.

2. Pour reserved tomato oil into pot. Place burgers into pot. Set to STOVETOP HIGH. Cook uncovered 2 minutes or until burgers are browned on both sides. Cover and cook 5 minutes or until burgers are cooked through. Remove burgers from pot and let stand 5 minutes.

3. Spread yogurt on top of buns. Place burgers on buns. Top with arugula.

NUTRITION PER SERVING: 390 CALORIES; 20G FAT; 6G SATURATED FAT; 440MG SODIUM; 23G CARBOHYDRATE; 2G FIBER; 29G PROTEIN

NINJA SERVING TIP

You can also use ground turkey instead of chicken and watercress in place of arugula.

SEARED SCALLOP SALAD WITH GRAPEFRUIT & AVOCADO

Thanks to the even heat in this pot, searing scallops is so easy. You will love the unexpected flavor combination of grapefruit, avocado, and honey.

PREP: 15 minutes • **COOK:** 6 minutes • **SERVINGS:** 4

Ingredients

1 grapefruit, cut in half and sectioned, reserving juice

1 avocado, pitted, peeled, and thinly sliced

1 shallot, minced

3 tablespoons honey

2 tablespoons white wine vinegar

1 tablespoon canola oil

Salt and ground black pepper

1 tablespoon butter

12 large sea scallops

1 head Boston or Bibb lettuce

Directions

1. Stir grapefruit sections and avocado in bowl. Stir reserved grapefruit juice, shallot, honey, vinegar, oil, salt, and black pepper in another bowl.

2. Add butter to pot. Set to STOVETOP HIGH and heat butter until melted and very hot. Add scallops to pot. Cook uncovered 6 minutes or until browned on both sides and cooked through, turning over once, halfway through cooking time.

3. Arrange lettuce on platter and top with grapefruit and avocado. Top with scallops and drizzle with grapefruit juice mixture.

NUTRITION PER SERVING: 280 CALORIES; 14G FAT; 3.5G SATURATED FAT; 100MG SODIUM; 28G CARBOHYDRATE; 5G FIBER; 10G PROTEIN

NINJA HEALTHY TIP

Use canola oil or reduced-fat butter instead of butter to sear scallops.

SEA BASS Á LA NAGE WITH STEAMED ROMAINE

This dish is healthful yet packed with flavor. The fish and romaine are layered in the pot and cook at the same time, while the sauce cooks in the bottom. It's perfect for a summer dinner party.

PREP: 20 minutes • **COOK:** 15 minutes • **SERVINGS:** 4

Ingredients

1 lemon

4 sea bass fillets, skin removed (about 1 pound)

Salt and ground black pepper

3 tablespoons butter

1 tablespoon minced shallot

2 garlic cloves, minced

½ cup white wine

½ cup chicken stock

2 hearts of romaine, cut in half lengthwise

2 teaspoons sliced fresh chives

Directions

1. Grate zest and squeeze juice from lemon. Season fish with salt and ground black pepper.

2. Place butter into pot. Set to STOVETOP HIGH and heat until butter is melted. Add shallot and garlic to pot. Cook uncovered 1 minute. Stir in wine and cook 2 minutes or until slightly reduced. Stir in stock and lemon zest and season with salt and black pepper.

3. Place fish on roasting rack and place rack into pot. Place romaine on top of fish. Season with salt and black pepper. Set OVEN to 425°F for 10 minutes. Cover and cook until fish flakes easily when tested with fork and romaine is tender-crisp.

4. Remove rack with fish and romaine from pot. Stir lemon juice into pot. Serve romaine topped with fish and drizzled with stock mixture. Sprinkle with chives.

NUTRITION PER SERVING: 230 CALORIES; 11G FAT; 6G SATURATED FAT; 210MG SODIUM; 4G CARBOHYDRATE; 1G FIBER; 22G PROTEIN

NINJA SERVING TIP

Use whichever white wine you prefer in this recipe, and serve the rest with dinner! Chardonnay will lend a more buttery flavor, while Riesling will add a sweeter, more fruity note.

Lite Fare

SAUTÉED CHICKEN BREASTS WITH CITRUS SALSA

Quick-cooking chicken seasoned in lime juice, then served with sweet and spicy salsa, will have your family calling for this great dish over and over.

PREP: 20 minutes • **COOK:** 20 minutes • **SERVINGS:** 4

Ingredients

1 large orange, cut in half and sectioned, reserving juice

1 medium grapefruit, cut in half and sectioned, reserving juice

⅓ cup chopped red onion

3 tablespoons lime juice

1 tablespoon chopped fresh cilantro leaves

½ jalapeño pepper, seeded and minced

1 tablespoon honey

1 tablespoon ground cumin

1 teaspoon ground coriander

½ teaspoon kosher salt

2 cloves garlic, minced

1 tablespoon canola oil

4 boneless, skinless chicken breast halves

Directions

1. Coarsely chop orange and grapefruit sections. Stir orange, grapefruit, reserved juices, onion, **1 tablespoon** lime juice, cilantro, jalapeño pepper, and honey in bowl.

2. Stir remaining lime juice, cumin, coriander, salt, and garlic in another bowl. Rub chicken with garlic mixture.

3. Pour oil into pot. Set to STOVETOP HIGH and heat oil. Add chicken and cook 12 minutes or until chicken is browned on both sides and cooked through, turning over once halfway through cooking time. Serve with citrus salsa.

NUTRITION PER SERVING: 250 CALORIES; 7G FAT; 1G SATURATED FAT; 310MG SODIUM; 18G CARBOHYDRATE; 2G FIBER; 28G PROTEIN

NINJA SERVING TIP

Serve with a fresh spinach salad with low-fat dressing.

 **STOVETOP/OVEN**

TURKEY CUTLETS WITH BRAISED FENNEL & ORANGE

Brown turkey cutlets, then braise fennel in honey-orange sauce — no need for a separate skillet and saucepan — it's all done in one pot!

PREP: 15 minutes • **COOK:** 45 minutes • **SERVINGS:** 6

Ingredients

1¾ pounds boneless turkey breast, sliced horizontally into ¼-inch thick fillets

Salt and ground black pepper

½ cup flour

3 tablespoons olive oil

2 fennel bulbs, cut into ½-inch slices

1½ cups orange juice

2 tablespoons honey

Directions

1. Season turkey with salt and black pepper. Coat turkey with flour.

2. Pour oil into pot. Set to STOVETOP HIGH and heat oil. Add turkey in batches to pot. Cook uncovered 10 minutes or until turkey is browned. Remove turkey from pot.

3. Add **half** the fennel to pot and season with salt and black pepper. Set to STOVETOP HIGH. Cook uncovered 5 minutes or until fennel is golden brown. Remove fennel from pot. Repeat with remaining fennel. Return cooked fennel to pot.

4. Add orange juice and honey to pot. Set OVEN to 250°F for 15 minutes. Cover and cook until fennel is tender, and orange juice mixture is reduced and thickened slightly.

5. Return turkey to pot and turn to coat. Set to STOVETOP HIGH. Cook uncovered 5 minutes or until turkey is cooked through, stirring occasionally.

NUTRITION PER SERVING:
300 CALORIES; 8G FAT; 1G SATURATED FAT; 90MG SODIUM; 27G CARBOHYDRATE; 3G FIBER; 30G PROTEIN

NINJA SERVING TIP

Add chopped fennel fronds and orange segments as a tasty and colorful garnish.

Lite Fare

VEGETARIAN MOUSSAKA

This layered casserole is Greek-style comfort food! Eggplant, tomatoes, zucchini, and potatoes are roasted in the pot until tender, then smothered in a cheesy cream sauce and baked — it's simply wonderful!

PREP: 20 minutes • **COOK:** 1 hour, 5 minutes • **SERVINGS:** 6

Ingredients

2 tablespoons olive oil

1 large eggplant, peeled and cut lengthwise into ¼-inch thick slices

1 can (14.5 ounces) diced tomatoes

½ teaspoon salt

⅛ teaspoon ground black pepper

¼ teaspoon ground cinnamon

2 large zucchini, cut lengthwise into ¼-inch-thick slices

1 can (15 ounces) sliced white potatoes, drained

1 cup tomato sauce

Gruyère Cream Sauce

Directions

1. Pour oil into pot. Arrange eggplant in pot. Set OVEN to 400°F for 15 minutes. Cover and cook 15 minutes or until eggplant is tender. Remove eggplant from pot.

2. Stir diced tomatoes, salt, black pepper, and cinnamon into pot. Layer **half** the zucchini, the eggplant, potatoes, and remaining zucchini in pot. Pour tomato sauce over zucchini. Set OVEN to 275°F for 50 minutes. Cover and cook 40 minutes.

3. Uncover and top with Gruyère Cream Sauce. Cover and cook 10 minutes or until cream sauce looks puffed.

4. For Gruyère Cream Sauce: Heat ¼ cup butter in saucepan over medium heat until melted. Stir in ¼ cup all-purpose flour and cook 2 minutes, stirring constantly. Stir in 1½ cups milk and heat to a boil. Reduce heat to low and cook 2 minutes. Stir in 1 cup shredded Gruyère or Swiss cheese, ½ teaspoon salt, and ½ teaspoon each ground black pepper and ground nutmeg. Stir in 1 beaten egg and cook 2 minutes or until mixture is thickened, stirring constantly.

NUTRITION PER SERVING:
350 CALORIES; 21G FAT;
10G SATURATED FAT; 960MG
SODIUM; 27G CARBOHYDRATE;
7G FIBER; 13G PROTEIN

 SERVING TIP

Add a green salad topped with feta cheese for a totally Greek meal.

COCONUT-CRUSTED TILAPIA WITH CARIBBEAN SALSA

This fresh-tasting dish is beautiful to look at and to eat, with golden-colored tilapia and colorful fruit salsa. It's good for you, too, since the fish is baked and not fried.

PREP: 15 minutes • **COOK:** 15 minutes • **SERVINGS:** 4

Ingredients

¼ cup Japanese-style bread crumbs (panko)

¼ cup shredded coconut, lightly toasted

1 tablespoon mayonnaise

1 tablespoon plus 1 teaspoon lime juice

½ teaspoon ground allspice

1 pound tilapia fillets

1 cup chopped mango

1 cup chopped pineapple

1 cup chopped red pepper

3 green onions, sliced

1 tablespoon chopped fresh cilantro leaves

½ teaspoon hot pepper sauce

Directions

1. Stir bread crumbs and coconut on plate. Stir mayonnaise, **1 teaspoon** lime juice, and allspice in bowl.

2. Place fish in shallow baking pan (7 x 10-inch), overlapping edges slightly to fit. Brush fish with mayonnaise mixture and sprinkle with bread crumb mixture.

3. Place wire rack into pot. Place pan on rack. Set OVEN to 425°F for 15 minutes. Cover and cook until fish flakes easily when tested with a fork.

4. Stir mango, pineapple, red pepper, green onions, cilantro, hot pepper sauce, and remaining lime juice in bowl. Serve mango mixture with fish.

NUTRITION PER SERVING: 250 CALORIES; 7G FAT; 2.5G SATURATED FAT; 110MG SODIUM; 21G CARBOHYDRATE; 3G FIBER; 25G PROTEIN

NINJA TIME-SAVER TIP

Get the pineapple and red pepper pre-cut at the grocery store salad bar to save on prep time.

PULLED PORK & APPLE CIDER SLIDERS • PAGE 50

CHAPTER 3:
Appetizers

 OVEN

BUFFALO CHICKEN POPPERS

These yummy snacks have all the flavor of buffalo chicken in one tiny little package that bakes perfectly in the pot! Chicken, hot pepper sauce, celery, and blue cheese wrapped in warm flaky crescent dough — they're irresistible!

PREP: 10 minutes • **COOK:** 10 minutes • **SERVINGS:** 8

Ingredients

¼ **cup butter, melted**

¼ **cup cayenne pepper sauce**

1 cup finely chopped rotisserie chicken

1 stalk celery, finely chopped

2 tablespoons crumbled blue cheese

1 package (8 ounces) refrigerated crescent rolls

Directions

1. Stir butter, pepper sauce, chicken, celery, and cheese in bowl.

2. Separate crescent rolls into **8** dough triangles, then cut triangles in half. Press down gently to flatten each triangle half. Place **2 tablespoons** chicken mixture in center of each triangle half. Pull one corner at a time up over the filling to enclose the filling.

3. Place filled dough into pot. Set OVEN to 375°F for 10 minutes. Cover and cook until poppers are golden brown, turning over once halfway through cooking time.

NINJA SERVING TIP

Serve with blue cheese or ranch dressing and cut-up celery for dipping.

STOVETOP/SLOW COOK

CAPONATA & GOAT CHEESE CROSTINI

Eggplant, onion, and garlic slow cook to melt-in-your-mouth tenderness, their rich flavor balanced by tart capers, creamy goat cheese, and crunchy pine nuts.

PREP: 15 minutes • **COOK:** 4 hours, 5 minutes • **SERVINGS:** 32

Ingredients

2 tablespoons olive oil

1 eggplant (about 2 pounds), unpeeled, cut into ½-inch pieces

1 medium onion, chopped

4 cloves garlic, chopped

1 can (29 ounces) diced tomatoes, undrained

2 tablespoons balsamic or red wine vinegar

¼ cup capers or chopped pitted oil-cured olives

2 baguettes, sliced and toasted

4 ounces crumbled goat cheese

Toasted pine nuts

Shredded fresh basil leaves

Directions

1. Place oil, eggplant, onion, and garlic into pot. Set to STOVETOP HIGH. Cook uncovered 5 minutes or until onion is tender, stirring occasionally.

2. Stir in tomatoes, vinegar, and capers. Set to SLOW COOK HIGH for 4 to 5 hours. Cover and cook until eggplant is very tender.

3. Stir eggplant mixture and serve on toasted baguette slices with goat cheese, pine nuts, and basil sprinkled on top.

NINJA SERVING TIP

Serve any leftover caponata over pasta for a quick and easy meatless meal.

STOVETOP/STEAM OVEN

CHICKEN & VEGETABLE SKEWERS WITH THAI COCONUT SAUCE

These wonderful little skewers are perfect for dipping and cook at the same time as the dipping sauce itself! Party-ready in no time.

PREP: 20 minutes • **COOK:** 15 minutes • **SERVINGS:** 8

Ingredients

1 lime

24 wooden picks

1 onion, cut into ½-inch pieces

1 pound skinless, boneless chicken breast halves, cut into 1-inch pieces

1 red pepper, cut into ½-inch pieces

Salt and ground black pepper

2 tablespoons canola oil

2 cloves garlic, minced

1 piece (1-inch) fresh ginger, peeled and minced

1 teaspoon red curry paste

1 can (13.5 ounces) coconut milk

2 tablespoons cornstarch

2 tablespoons cold water

Fresh cilantro leaves

Directions

1. Grate zest and squeeze juice from lime.

2. Thread **1 piece** onion, **1 piece** chicken, and **1 piece** red pepper on **each** wooden pick. Season with salt and black pepper.

3. Stir oil, garlic, ginger, and curry paste into pot. Set to STOVETOP HIGH. Cook uncovered 2 minutes or until garlic and ginger are tender, stirring occasionally. Stir in coconut milk and lime zest. Season with salt and black pepper.

4. Place skewers on roasting rack. Place roasting rack into pot. Set OVEN to 350°F for 10 minutes. Cover and cook until chicken is cooked through. Remove skewers and rack from pot.

5. Stir cornstarch, water, and lime juice in bowl. Stir cornstarch mixture into pot. Set to STOVETOP HIGH. Cook uncovered 2 minutes or until mixture is thickened, stirring constantly. Season with salt and black pepper.

6. Serve skewers with coconut sauce. Garnish with cilantro leaves.

NINJA SERVING TIP

Toss leftover Thai coconut sauce with cilantro and cooked soba noodles or linguine for lunch the next day.

 **STOVETOP/OVEN**

SAUSAGE-STUFFED BABY PORTOBELLO MUSHROOMS

This classic dish for entertaining has never been easier to make. Cook sausage filling, then bake the stuffed mushrooms in the same pot!

PREP: 20 minutes • **COOK:** 35 minutes • **SERVINGS:** 7

Ingredients

1 package (16 ounces) baby portobello mushrooms

1 package (12 ounces) mild Italian sausage, casing removed

1 small green or red pepper, chopped

1 small onion, chopped

1 stalk celery, chopped

2 cloves garlic, minced

¼ cup Italian-seasoned dry bread crumbs

¼ cup grated Parmesan cheese

⅛ teaspoon ground black pepper

Directions

1. Separate mushroom stems from mushroom caps. **Reserve** mushroom caps. Finely chop mushroom stems to make ½ cup.

2. Place sausage, green pepper, onion, celery, chopped mushroom stems, and garlic into pot. Set to STOVETOP HIGH. Cook uncovered 12 minutes or until sausage is cooked through and vegetables are tender, stirring occasionally.

3. Turn off pot. Stir in bread crumbs, **2 tablespoons** cheese, and black pepper. Spoon filling mixture into reserved mushroom caps. Place stuffed mushrooms on roasting rack.

4. Wipe inside of pot with paper towel. Place rack into pot. Set OVEN to 425°F for 25 minutes. Cover and cook until mushrooms are tender. Sprinkle with remaining Parmesan cheese.

NINJA SERVING TIP

For a zestier filling, use hot Italian sausage instead of mild.

Appetizers

KOREAN CHICKEN WINGS

The blend of soy sauce, brown sugar, garlic, and ginger doesn't only coat these wings; slow cooking intensifies the flavor and helps permeate the meat, making the wings delicious through and through.

PREP: 10 minutes • **COOK:** 3 hours, 5 minutes • **SERVINGS:** 4

Ingredients

2 pounds chicken wings, tips removed

½ cup soy sauce

¼ cup packed brown sugar

3 cloves garlic, minced

2 tablespoons peeled, chopped fresh ginger

3 green onions, thinly sliced

Directions

1. Set pot to STOVETOP HIGH. Add chicken to pot. Cook uncovered 5 minutes or until chicken is lightly browned on both sides.

2. Stir soy sauce, brown sugar, garlic, ginger, and green onions in bowl. Pour soy sauce mixture over chicken and toss to coat. Set to SLOW COOK LOW for 3 to 5 hours. Cover and cook until chicken is cooked through.

 SERVING TIP

Double the recipe for a great party dish and keep warm in pot on SLOW COOK BUFFET.

SLOW COOK

Signature

PULLED PORK & APPLE CIDER SLIDERS

Slow cooking guarantees tender pork. Braised with cider and spicy mustard, these pulled pork sliders make indulgent little sandwiches that are perfect served with baked sweet potato fries.

PREP: 10 minutes • **COOK:** 5 hours • **SERVINGS:** 6

Ingredients

1 boneless pork shoulder roast
(3 to 4 pounds)

Salt and ground black pepper

2 teaspoons paprika

¼ cup spicy brown mustard

¼ cup packed brown sugar

3 cloves garlic, minced

1 cup apple cider or apple juice

1 package (15 ounces) slider or mini
sandwich buns (12 mini buns)

Directions

1. Season pork with salt, black pepper, and paprika. Stir mustard, brown sugar, garlic, and cider in pot. Add pork and turn to coat. Set to SLOW-COOK HIGH for 5 to 6 hours. Cover and cook until pork is fork-tender.

2. Using two forks, shred pork in pot. Spread additional mustard on buns, if desired. Divide pork mixture among buns.

NINJA TIME-SAVER TIP

Keep this meal quick and simple and serve with sweet potato fries from the freezer section and sliced fresh cucumber with ranch dressing for dipping.

 STOVETOP/STEAM OVEN

SPICY MUSSELS

Treat yourself to these amazing mussels, cooked in a fennel-white wine broth. The mussels steam in the pot with the broth, infusing them with flavor.

PREP: 10 minutes • **COOK:** 20 minutes • **SERVINGS:** 6

Ingredients

2 tablespoons olive oil

1 small onion, chopped

½ small fennel bulb, chopped (about 2 cups)

½ teaspoon salt

3 cloves garlic, minced

1 cup white wine

1 cup vegetable broth

½ teaspoon crushed red pepper

2 pounds mussels, scrubbed

1 tablespoon fresh chopped parsley

Directions

1. Pour oil into pot. Set to STOVETOP HIGH and heat oil. Add onion, fennel, and salt to pot. Cook uncovered 10 minutes or until vegetables are very tender, stirring occasionally. Stir in garlic. Cook 1 minute, stirring often. Stir in wine, broth, and red pepper.

2. Place mussels on wire rack. Place rack into pot. Set OVEN to 350°F for 10 minutes. Cover and cook until mussels are cooked. Place mussels into serving bowl. Stir parsley into broth mixture and pour broth mixture over mussels.

 SERVING TIP

Serve this dish with crusty bread for dipping in the savory broth.

STOVETOP

PRETZEL-COATED CHICKEN TENDERS

This twist on chicken fingers features a crunchy pretzel coating and a decadent cheesy sauce for dipping. The chicken cooks up crisp on the outside and juicy on the inside, and you make the sauce in the pot, too! Only one pot to clean!

PREP: 10 minutes • **COOK:** 15 minutes • **SERVINGS:** 8

Ingredients

1 egg

2 cups butter-flavored pretzels, finely crushed

1 pound boneless chicken breast tenderloins

2 tablespoons vegetable oil

¾ cup beer or chicken broth

½ of a 16-ounce package pasteurized prepared cheese product, cut up

1 teaspoon Worcestershire sauce

1 teaspoon spicy brown mustard

Directions

1. Beat egg in shallow dish. Pour pretzel crumbs onto plate. Dip chicken into egg. Coat chicken with pretzel crumbs.

2. Pour oil into pot. Set to STOVETOP HIGH and heat oil. Add chicken to pot. Cook uncovered 10 minutes or until chicken is browned on both sides and cooked through. Remove chicken from pot, lightly cover, and keep warm.

3. Pour beer into pot and heat to a boil. Add cheese, Worcestershire sauce, and mustard. Cook uncovered until cheese is melted and mixture is smooth, stirring often. Serve sauce with chicken.

NINJA SERVING TIP

Try cutting the chicken into bite-sized pieces before coating and cooking, then serve on a platter with wooden picks.

STOVETOP/SLOW COOK

BROCCOLI CHEESE DIP

This is no ordinary broccoli dip! Sautéed onion provides a savory base, then broccoli, cheese, and seasonings slow cook until the mixture is hot and the flavors are blended. A bit of sun-dried tomato pesto adds the perfect tasty twist.

PREP: 10 minutes • **COOK:** 2 hours, 10 minutes • **SERVINGS:** 6

Ingredients

1 tablespoon olive oil

1 medium onion, chopped

4 cups chopped fresh broccoli

1 can (10¾ ounces) condensed broccoli cheese soup

½ cup milk

1 tablespoon Worcestershire sauce

1 tablespoon sun-dried tomato pesto sauce

1 cup shredded Cheddar cheese

Ground black pepper

Directions

1. Pour oil into pot. Set to STOVETOP HIGH and heat oil. Add onion to pot. Cook uncovered 5 minutes or until onion is tender-crisp, stirring occasionally. Add broccoli to pot. Cook 5 minutes, stirring occasionally.

2. Stir soup, milk, Worcestershire sauce, pesto sauce, cheese, and black pepper into pot. Set to SLOW COOK LOW for 2 hours. Cover and cook until broccoli is tender and cheese is melted.

NINJA HEALTHY TIP

Substitute reduced-fat broccoli cheese soup and 2% milk Cheddar cheese for the versions in the recipe.

CHICKEN TORTILLA SOUP • PAGE 59

CHAPTER 4:
Soups/ Stews

STOVETOP/SLOW COOK

BUTTERNUT SQUASH & APPLE SOUP

This soup tastes decadent but is packed with nutrients and fiber. Using a hand blender or immersion blender for the last step keeps it all in one pot!

PREP: 15 minutes • **COOK:** 1 hour, 10 minutes • **SERVINGS:** 6

Ingredients

2 tablespoons butter

1 package (20 ounces) fresh peeled, cubed butternut squash (about 4 cups)

1 large onion, chopped

1 large Granny Smith apple, peeled, cored, and chopped

¼ teaspoon pumpkin pie spice or ground cinnamon

1 teaspoon salt

¼ teaspoon ground black pepper

3 cups chicken broth

2 bay leaves

¼ cup half-and-half

Directions

1. Place butter, squash, onion, and apple into pot. Set to STOVETOP HIGH. Cook uncovered 10 minutes or until squash is lightly browned, stirring occasionally. Stir in pumpkin pie spice, salt, and black pepper.

2. Add broth and bay leaves. Set to SLOW COOK HIGH for 1 to 2 hours. Cover and cook until squash is tender.

3. Remove and discard bay leaves. Purée soup mixture using immersion blender directly in pot or carefully pour hot soup mixture into regular blender in batches and purée soup until smooth. Stir in half-and-half.

NINJA SERVING TIP

Top each serving with sautéed fresh sage leaves: Heat 1 tablespoon olive oil in skillet over medium-high heat. Add ¼ cup fresh sage leaves. Cook 1 minute, turning once. Carefully remove leaves and drain on paper towels.

STOVETOP/SLOW COOK

WHITE TURKEY CHILI

Browning turkey and sausage adds an extra dimension of flavor to this wholesome chili — and there's no extra skillet to clean!

PREP: 30 minutes • **COOK:** 7 hours • **SERVINGS:** 8

Ingredients

1 can (7 ounces) chipotle peppers in adobo sauce

2 tablespoons olive oil

1 pound ground turkey or chicken

1 pound Italian-style turkey sausage, casing removed

1 small white onion, diced

1 can (4.25 ounces) diced green chiles

2 cans (15.5 ounces each) cannellini beans, drained and rinsed

2½ cups chicken stock

1 clove garlic, chopped

½ teaspoon cayenne pepper

2 tablespoons chili powder

1½ teaspoons ground cumin

½ cup frozen corn

Directions

1. Finely chop **half** of the chipotle pepper and reserve **1 teaspoon** adobo sauce.

2. Pour **1 tablespoon** oil into pot. Set to STOVETOP HIGH and heat oil. Add turkey to pot. Cook uncovered until turkey is browned, stirring often. Add sausage and remaining oil to pot. Cook uncovered until sausage is browned, stirring often.

3. Stir chipotle pepper, reserved adobo sauce, onion, green chiles, beans, stock, garlic, cayenne pepper, chili powder, and cumin into pot. Set to SLOW COOK LOW for 7 to 9 hours. Cover and cook, stirring in corn during last 30 minutes of cooking time.

 SERVING TIP

Top with a lime crema (sour cream and lime juice), diced avocado, diced red or yellow peppers, or cilantro as desired.

STOVETOP/SLOW COOK

Signature

CHICKEN TORTILLA SOUP

This flavorful soup yields hearty bowlfuls of shredded chicken, tomatoes, beans, corn, and tortilla strips. Browning the chicken, then slow simmering in the pot locks in the flavor.

PREP: 20 minutes • **COOK:** 2 hours, 5 minutes • **SERVINGS:** 8

Ingredients

1 tablespoon canola oil

1¼ pounds boneless, skinless chicken breast halves

1 medium onion, chopped

2 cloves garlic, chopped

¼ cup fresh cilantro leaves, chopped

2 cans (14.5 ounces each) diced tomatoes, undrained

2 cans (10 ounces each) enchilada sauce

1 can (14.5 ounces) low-sodium chicken broth

1 can (about 15 ounces) black beans, undrained

1 package (10 ounces) frozen corn, thawed

1 tablespoon each chili powder and ground cumin

5 corn tortillas (6-inch), cut into 3-inch x ½-inch strips

Directions

1. Pour oil into pot. Set to STOVETOP MED and heat oil. Add chicken to pot. Cook uncovered 5 minutes or until chicken is lightly browned on both sides.

2. Stir onion, garlic, cilantro, tomatoes, enchilada sauce, broth, beans, corn, chili powder, and cumin in pot. Set to SLOW COOK HIGH for 2 to 3 hours. Cover and cook until chicken is fork-tender.

3. Using 2 forks, shred chicken in pot. Top soup with tortillas before serving.

NINJA SERVING TIP

This soup is delicious served with diced avocado sprinkled on top with the tortillas.

STOVETOP/SLOW COOK

CHILI WITH CORN BREAD CRUST

Spicy red chili with beans simmers in pot, then corn bread batter is spooned on top. The corn bread bakes right on top of the chili — this main dish and side dish in one is perfect for a cold winter night!

PREP: 20 minutes • **COOK:** 4 hours, 10 minutes • **SERVINGS:** 6

Ingredients

1 tablespoon vegetable oil

1½ pounds ground beef or turkey

1 large onion, diced

1 green pepper, diced

1 tablespoon chili powder

½ teaspoon ground cinnamon

1 can (28 ounces) diced tomatoes, undrained

1 can (about 15 ounces) kidney beans, rinsed and drained

1 tablespoon tomato paste

1 package (8.5 ounces) corn muffin mix

1 egg, beaten

⅓ cup milk

Directions

1. Pour oil into pot. Set to STOVETOP HIGH and heat oil. Add beef, onion, and pepper to pot. Cook uncovered 10 minutes or until beef is browned, stirring occasionally. Spoon off any fat. Add chili powder and cinnamon to pot. Cook 5 minutes, stirring occasionally.

2. Stir tomatoes, beans, and tomato paste in pot. Set to SLOW COOK HIGH for 4 to 5 hours. Cover and cook.

3. After 4½ hours of cooking time, stir muffin mix, egg, and milk in bowl. Uncover pot and spoon batter over chili. Cover and cook 30 minutes or until corn bread is cooked through.

NINJA SERVING TIP

Serve with sour cream and shredded Cheddar cheese.

STOVETOP/SLOW COOK

CREAMY CORN CHOWDER

Consistent heat from our pot makes from-scratch sauces simple. Add potatoes, corn, and broth and it's hands-free slow cooking to the finish.

PREP: 10 minutes • **COOK:** 4 hours, 5 minutes • **SERVINGS:** 6

Ingredients

2 tablespoons olive oil

1 medium onion, chopped

2 cloves garlic, chopped

8 ounces thick-sliced ham, cut into ¼-inch pieces

3 tablespoons all-purpose flour

1 large unpeeled russet potato, cut into ½-inch pieces

1 package (12 ounces) frozen corn, thawed

4 cups chicken broth

1 cup heavy cream

Oyster crackers

Directions

1. Place oil, onion, garlic, and ham in pot. Set to STOVETOP HIGH. Cook uncovered 3 minutes or until onion is tender, stirring occasionally. Stir in flour. Cook uncovered 1 minute, stirring constantly.

2. Add potato, corn, and broth to pot. Set to SLOW COOK HIGH for 4 to 5 hours. Cover and cook until potato is tender. Stir in cream and serve with crackers.

NINJA TIME-SAVER TIP

Substitute 8 ounces chopped, cooked bacon for ham.

STOVETOP/SLOW COOK

FRENCH ONION SOUP

Simple ingredients meet to make a sublime version of this classic soup. Onions are caramelized right in the pot, then finished on slow cook in the herb-brandy broth until silky.

PREP: 10 minutes • **COOK:** 1 hour, 16 minutes • **SERVINGS:** 4

Ingredients

¼ cup butter

2 large onions, thinly sliced

6 sprigs fresh thyme

1½ tablespoons chopped fresh rosemary leaves

Salt and ground black pepper

¾ cup brandy

¼ cup all-purpose flour

1 package (32 ounces) beef stock

12 oven-baked garlic Italian toasts

½ pound shredded Gruyère cheese

Directions

1. Place butter into pot. Set to STOVETOP HIGH. Heat uncovered until butter is melted. Add onions, thyme, rosemary, salt, and black pepper. Cook uncovered 15 minutes or until onions are very tender, stirring occasionally. Stir in brandy and flour. Cook uncovered 1 minute or until mixture is thickened, stirring constantly.

2. Pour stock into pot. Season with salt and black pepper. Set to SLOW COOK HIGH for 1 to 2 hours. Cover and cook.

3. Place 3 toasts in each of 4 bowls. Sprinkle with cheese. Spoon soup over cheese-topped toasts.

NINJA SERVING TIP

If you can't find Italian toasts, use garlic or other purchased croutons.

SMOKY NEW ENGLAND CLAM CHOWDER

Poach clams and make homemade clam broth. Then move along to slow cook this hearty chowder all in the same pot!

PREP: 15 minutes • **COOK:** 2 hours • **SERVINGS:** 6

Ingredients

3 cups chicken broth

3 dozen littleneck clams, scrubbed

4 slices bacon

2 pounds white potatoes, peeled and cut into cubes

1 large sweet onion, chopped

2 stalks celery, thinly sliced

2 tablespoons all-purpose flour

2 small bay leaves

1 cup light cream

1 teaspoon salt

¼ teaspoon white pepper

2 tablespoons finely chopped parsley

Directions

1. Add **1 cup** chicken broth and clams to pot. Set to STOVETOP HIGH. Cover and cook 10 minutes or until clams are cooked. Remove clams and broth. Remove clams from shells, reserving 8 for garnish. Refrigerate clams. Strain broth mixture and reserve.

2. Add bacon to pot. Set to STOVETOP HIGH. Cook uncovered 10 minutes or until bacon is crisp, stirring occasionally. Drain bacon on paper towels and crumble.

3. Add potatoes, onion, and celery to pot. Cook uncovered 10 minutes or until tender, stirring occasionally. Stir in flour. Cook uncovered 2 minutes, stirring often. Stir in remaining chicken broth, reserved broth mixture, and bay leaves. Set to SLOW COOK HIGH for 1 to 2 hours. Cover and cook.

4. Discard bay leaves. Lightly mash potatoes in soup. Stir in reserved clams, cream, salt, and pepper. Set to SLOW COOK HIGH for 30 minutes. Cover and cook until soup is hot. Stir in parsley. Top each serving with clam in shell, bacon, and parsley.

NINJA HEALTHY TIP

Substitute fat-free low-sodium chicken broth for regular broth and fat-free half-and-half for light cream.

STOVETOP/SLOW COOK

SWEET POTATO LENTIL SOUP

This soup is packed with fiber and vitamins. Who knew eating well could be so delicious? Onion and garlic are sautéed in the pot, then sweet potatoes, lentils, and chickpeas slow simmer until dinnertime.

PREP: 15 minutes • **COOK:** 7 hours, 5 minutes • **SERVINGS:** 10

Ingredients

2 tablespoons olive oil

1 large onion, chopped

3 cloves garlic, minced

1 large carrot, peeled and chopped

1 large sweet potato, peeled and cut into cubes

8 cups chicken broth

2 cups dried lentils

1 can (14.5 ounces) diced tomatoes

1 teaspoon dried oregano leaves, crushed

1 teaspoon salt

¼ teaspoon ground black pepper

1 can (about 15 ounces) chickpeas (garbanzo beans), undrained

Directions

1. Pour oil into pot. Set to STOVETOP HIGH and heat oil. Add onion and garlic to pot. Cook uncovered 5 minutes or until onion is tender, stirring occasionally.

2. Stir carrot, sweet potato, broth, lentils, tomatoes, oregano, salt, and black pepper into pot. Set to SLOW COOK LOW for 7 hours. Cover and cook until vegetables are tender. Stir in chickpeas during last 30 minutes of cooking time.

NINJA SERVING TIP

Stir ¼ cup finely chopped fresh parsley, 1 tablespoon grated lemon zest, and 1 clove garlic, minced in bowl. Sprinkle mixture over soup before serving. Finish with a drizzle of olive oil.

 **STOVETOP/SLOW COOK**

Signature

HEARTY BEEF STEW

Why brown and braise the beef in the same pot? You keep all the rich flavor of the browning, and it makes cleanup a breeze. This recipe adds the convenience of the slow cooker — no tending needed!

PREP: 10 minutes • **COOK:** 7 hours, 10 minutes • **SERVINGS:** 8

Ingredients

2 pounds beef for stew

1 teaspoon salt

½ teaspoon ground black pepper

¼ cup all-purpose flour

2 tablespoons vegetable oil

1½ cups beef broth

4 red potatoes, cut in half

2 onions, cut in quarters

1 cup baby carrots

4 cloves garlic, chopped

2 sprigs fresh thyme or 1 teaspoon dried thyme leaves, crushed

1 cup frozen peas, thawed

Directions

1. Season beef with salt and black pepper. Coat with flour.

2. Pour oil into pot. Set to STOVETOP HIGH and heat oil. Add beef and cook uncovered 10 minutes or until browned, stirring occasionally.

3. Stir broth, potatoes, onions, carrots, garlic, and thyme in pot. Set to SLOW COOK LOW for 7 to 9 hours. Cover and cook until beef is fork-tender. Stir in peas during last 10 minutes of cooking time.

 **NINJA** TIME-SAVER TIP

You can reduce the SLOW COOK step by slow cooking on HIGH for 4 hours.

DRY-RUBBED ROASTED TURKEY TENDERLOINS WITH SWEET CHILI • PAGE 80

CHAPTER 5:
Entrees

STOVETOP/SLOW COOK

SAVORY POT ROAST

This recipe elevates an inexpensive cut of meat to something worthy of a special meal. Browning beef first is essential to creating the rich flavor base, and now you can do it all in the same pot.

PREP: 20 minutes • **COOK:** 6 hours, 25 minutes • **SERVINGS:** 8

Ingredients

1 boneless beef chuck roast
 (3 to 4 pounds)

¼ cup plus 2 tablespoons flour

¼ cup olive oil

2 carrots, peeled and chopped

2 stalks celery, chopped

1 medium onion, chopped

3 cloves garlic, crushed

1 can (28 ounces) whole plum
 tomatoes in purée

1 cup each red wine and beef broth

3 sprigs fresh thyme

2 sprigs fresh rosemary

1 tablespoon butter, softened

Directions

1. Coat beef with ¼ **cup** flour.

2. Pour **half** of oil into pot. Set to STOVETOP HIGH and heat oil. Add beef to pot. Cook uncovered 10 minutes or until browned on all sides. Remove beef from pot.

3. Add remaining oil, carrots, celery, onion, and garlic to pot. Cook uncovered 10 minutes or until vegetables are tender, stirring occasionally. Add tomatoes, wine, broth, thyme, and rosemary and heat to a boil.

4. Return beef to pot. Set to SLOW COOK LOW for 6 to 8 hours. Cover and cook until beef is fork-tender.

5. Remove beef to cutting board. Stir butter and remaining flour in bowl. Stir butter mixture into pot. Set to STOVETOP HIGH. Cook uncovered 2 minutes or until gravy is thickened. Serve beef with gravy.

 TIME-SAVER TIP

Cook pot roast in about half the time: Set pot to SLOW COOK HIGH for 4 to 5 hours.

STOVETOP/STEAM OVEN

PRIME RIB AU JUS

Searing the beef in the pot first ensures a flavorful crust that tastes great and helps to seal in the juices. Finish cooking the beef, then use the drippings to create a rich, meaty au jus. A special-occasion main dish, and only one pot to clean!

PREP: 10 minutes • **COOK:** 1 hour, 30 minutes • **SERVINGS:** 4

Ingredients

1 beef standing rib roast (about 5 pounds)

Salt and ground black pepper

1 tablespoon chopped fresh rosemary leaves

4 cups beef broth

1 tablespoon butter, softened

1 tablespoon all-purpose flour

Directions

1. Season beef with salt, black pepper, and rosemary. Set pot to STOVETOP HIGH and heat pan. Add beef and cook uncovered 10 minutes or until browned on all sides. Remove beef from pot.

2. Pour broth into pot. Place roasting rack into pot. Place beef on rack. Set OVEN to 350°F for 1 hour. Cover and cook 1 hour for medium-rare or until desired doneness. Remove beef to cutting board and cover with foil.

3. Stir butter and flour in bowl. Add butter mixture to pot. Set to STOVETOP HIGH. Cook 10 minutes or until mixture is slightly reduced, stirring constantly. Serve sauce with beef.

NINJA SERVING TIP

Serve with garlic mashed potatoes and creamed spinach for a real steakhouse-style dinner!

STOVETOP/OVEN

Signature

UPSIDE-DOWN MAC & CHEESE

A macaroni and cheese version of spaghetti pie, this recipe features cheese-sauced pasta baked in a Cheddar bread crumb crust. Everything is cooked in the same pot for easy cleanup.

PREP: 15 minutes • **COOK:** 20 minutes • **SERVINGS:** 8

Ingredients

4 cups water

1 pound uncooked elbow macaroni

¾ cup butter

6 tablespoons all-purpose flour

5 cups whole milk

6¾ cups shredded extra-sharp Cheddar cheese

½ cup grated Pecorino Romano or Parmesan cheese

Salt and ground black pepper

Cooking spray

1½ cups bread crumbs

Directions

1. Pour water into pot. Set to STOVETOP HIGH. Heat uncovered to a boil. Stir in macaroni. Cook uncovered 9 minutes or until macaroni is just tender, stirring occasionally. Remove macaroni from pot and drain well in colander, reserving **1 cup** cooking water.

2. Add **½ cup** butter to pot. Set to STOVETOP MED and heat until butter is melted. Stir in flour. Cook uncovered 3 minutes, stirring constantly. Add milk and heat to a boil, stirring constantly. Cook uncovered 3 minutes, or until mixture is thickened and smooth, stirring occasionally. Stir in **6 cups** Cheddar cheese, **¼ cup** Pecorino Romano cheese, salt, and pepper until cheeses are melted, stirring occasionally. Turn off pot.

3. Stir cheese mixture, macaroni, and reserved cooking water in large bowl. Wipe pot clean.

4. Melt remaining ¼ cup butter. Stir melted butter, bread crumbs, ¾ cup Cheddar cheese, and ¼ cup Pecorino Romano in bowl.

5. Spray pot with cooking spray. Press bread crumb mixture onto bottom and 1 inch up sides of pot. Pour in macaroni mixture. Set OVEN to 350°F for 20 minutes, checking after 15 minutes. Cook until golden brown on bottom and sides and invert onto plate.

NINJA HEALTHY TIP

Serve with sliced fresh tomato salad.

STOVETOP/STEAM OVEN

Signature

SWEET & SPICY PORK BABY BACK RIBS

Browning the ribs in the pot seals in the flavor of the smoky-sweet spice rub, then steam roasting cooks the ribs until the meat is falling off the bone. Glazing with barbecue sauce to finish adds an extra layer of flavor.

PREP: 10 minutes • **COOK:** 1 hour, 40 minutes • **SERVINGS:** 4

Ingredients

1 tablespoon smoked paprika

1 tablespoon packed brown sugar

⅛ teaspoon cayenne pepper

1 rack pork baby back ribs (about 3 pounds), cut in half

Salt and ground black pepper

1 tablespoon vegetable oil

3 cups beef broth or water

½ cup barbecue sauce

Directions

1. Stir paprika, brown sugar, and cayenne pepper in bowl. Rub ribs with paprika mixture. Season with salt and black pepper.

2. Pour oil into pot. Set to STOVETOP HIGH and heat oil. Add **half** the ribs to pot. Cook uncovered 5 minutes or until browned on both sides. Remove ribs from pot. Repeat with remaining ribs. Remove ribs from pot.

3. Pour broth into pot. Place roasting rack into pot. Place ribs on rack. Set OVEN to 375°F for 1 hour. Cover and cook until pork is fork-tender.

4. Uncover pot and brush ribs with sauce. Set OVEN to 375°F for 30 minutes. Cover and cook until sauce is hot.

NINJA SERVING TIP

After cooking, cut ribs in-between bones for easy serving.

 STOVETOP/STEAM OVEN

GARLIC-INFUSED CHUCK ROAST

Searing and steam roasting a chuck roast makes it as tender and juicy as roast beef. The garlic is placed alongside the roast and cooks simultaneously, becoming sweet and succulent.

PREP: 1 minute • **COOK:** 1 hour, 30 minutes • **SERVINGS:** 6–8

Ingredients

4-4½ pounds chuck roast, tied

1 tablespoon plus 1 teaspoon canola oil

½ teaspoon salt

¼ teaspoon cayenne

¼ teaspoon black pepper

¼ teaspoon garlic powder or granulated garlic

4 cups beef broth

1½ cups red wine

2 garlic bulbs, cut ¼ inch (on root end) across top

Directions

1. Rub chuck roast with **1 tablespoon** canola oil and season meat with salt and pepper. Set to STOVETOP HIGH and sear meat on all sides.

2. Remove meat and sprinkle seared meat with garlic powder and cayenne.

3. Add broth and red wine to pot, place roasting rack in pot, and place meat on rack. Set OVEN to 350°F for 55 minutes. Place both prepped garlic heads in the cooker on the sides of the meat and drizzle with 1 teaspoon of oil. Cover and cook until the internal temperature of meat registers 120°F for medium (light pink) and 145°F for medium-well. (Meat internal temperature will continue to rise after cooking approximately 20°F)

4. Remove rack, meat, and garlic heads. While roast is resting, squeeze garlic out from both garlic bulbs and spread thinly on top of the resting roast.

5. Thinly slice beef topped with roasted garlic and drizzle with sauce.

NINJA SERVING TIP

For sauce: Combine 2 tablespoons cornstarch with 2 tablespoons water and pour into broth in bottom of pot, bring to a boil, and boil for 5 minutes, whisking constantly. Turn off heat and whisk in 2 tablespoons cold, diced butter until melted.

STOVETOP/STEAM OVEN

Signature

LEMON CHICKEN WITH ROSEMARY

Fresh lemon and rosemary complement the richly roasted flavor of the chicken, made moist and tender using this foolproof cooking method.

PREP: 15 minutes • **COOK:** 1 hour, 15 minutes • **SERVINGS:** 6

Ingredients

1 lemon

3 sprigs fresh rosemary

6 pound whole roasting chicken

Salt and ground black pepper

2 large onions, sliced

3 cloves garlic, sliced

4 cups chicken broth

Directions

1. Grate and reserve **1 tablespoon** zest from lemon. Cut lemon in quarters. Chop and reserve **1 sprig** rosemary.

2. Remove package of giblets and neck from chicken cavities. Rinse chicken and pat dry with paper towel. Place lemon quarters and remaining rosemary sprigs into chicken cavity. Season chicken with salt and pepper.

3. Set to STOVETOP HIGH. Place chicken into pot. Cook uncovered, searing chicken for approximately 5 to 7 minutes on each side as desired. Remove chicken from pot and place on roasting rack.

4. Place onions, garlic, and broth into pot. Place rack with chicken in pot. Sprinkle chicken with reserved lemon zest and chopped rosemary. Set OVEN to 375°F for 1 hour and 15 minutes. Cover and cook until chicken is cooked through and juices run clear.

NINJA TIME-SAVER TIP

Use leftovers from this delicious chicken for two or more meals later in the week. Great for lunch with mixed salad greens, chopped fresh vegetables, and low-fat dressing.

 STOVETOP

SHRIMP & BROCCOLI SAUTÉ

Skip the thawing step with this twist on traditional scampi. Frozen shrimp, broccoli, and peas cook quickly in a lemony sauce, then are tossed with pasta and sprinkled with crunchy pine nuts.

PREP: 20 minutes • **COOK:** 25 minutes • **SERVINGS:** 4

Ingredients

1 lemon

1 tablespoon olive oil

1 large onion, sliced

3 cloves garlic, minced

1 teaspoon salt

½ teaspoon ground black pepper

1 pound uncooked frozen jumbo shrimp, peeled and deveined (about 16 per pound)

1 pound broccoli, cut into thin spears, or 1 package (16 ounces) frozen cut-up broccoli

½ cup frozen peas

1 can (14.5 ounces) chicken broth

¼ teaspoon crushed red pepper

½ of a 1-pound package linguine pasta, cooked and drained

⅓ cup toasted pine nuts

Directions

1. Grate **1 teaspoon** zest from lemon.

2. Pour oil into pot. Set to STOVETOP HIGH and heat oil. Add onion to pot. Cook uncovered 5 minutes or until onion is tender, stirring occasionally. Add garlic, salt, black pepper, and shrimp to pot. Cook 2 minutes, stirring often.

3. Stir in broccoli, peas, broth, red pepper, and lemon zest and heat to a boil. Cook 5 minutes or until broccoli is tender-crisp and shrimp are cooked through, stirring occasionally. Serve shrimp mixture over pasta and sprinkle with pine nuts.

NINJA SERVING TIP

This brothy dish would also be delicious served over hot cooked white rice instead of pasta.

 **SLOW COOK**

CORNED BEEF & CABBAGE

Don't wait for holiday time to make this delicious one-pot meal! It's so easy anytime you want something comforting — brisket, potatoes, vegetables, and spices slow cook with no tending.

PREP: 15 minutes • **COOK:** 4 hours, 40 minutes • **SERVINGS:** 6

Ingredients

2 celery stalks, cut into 3-inch pieces

1 cup baby carrots

1 onion, cut into wedges

6 small potatoes, cut in half

6 sprigs thyme or 1 teaspoon dried thyme leaves, crushed

1 corned beef brisket (about 4 pounds) with pickling spice packet

½ head green cabbage, cut into wedges

Directions

1. Place celery, carrots, onion, potatoes, thyme, and pickling spice into pot. Place beef into pot, fat side up. Add enough water to almost cover beef. Set to SLOW COOK HIGH for 4 to 5 hours. Cover and cook until beef is fork-tender.

2. Arrange cabbage over beef. Set to SLOW COOK HIGH for 40 minutes. Cover and cook until cabbage is tender.

 SERVING TIP

Cook brisket on LOW setting for 7 to 9 hours and 1 hour for cabbage if timing works better for meal planning. Serve with grainy mustard.

STOVETOP/OVEN

DRY-RUBBED ROASTED TURKEY TENDERLOINS WITH SWEET CHILI

A spiced, sweet dry rub seasons the turkey before it's seared in the pot. It's pan-roasting, but with an all-in-one appliance that doesn't heat up your kitchen!

PREP: 10 minutes • **COOK:** 30 minutes • **SERVINGS:** 6

Ingredients

1 tablespoon sugar

1 teaspoon salt

1 teaspoon ground cinnamon

1 teaspoon garlic powder

½ teaspoon dried thyme leaves, crushed

¼ teaspoon ground cumin

1 package (24 ounces) boneless turkey breast tenderloins

2 tablespoons olive oil

⅓ cup sweet chili sauce

1 teaspoon Worcestershire sauce

Directions

1. Stir sugar, salt, cinnamon, garlic powder, thyme, and cumin in bowl. Brush turkey with **1 tablespoon** oil. Rub turkey with sugar mixture.

2. Pour remaining oil into pot. Set to STOVETOP HIGH and heat oil. Add turkey to pot. Cook uncovered 15 minutes or until browned on both sides. Remove turkey from pot.

3. Place roasting rack into pot. Place turkey on rack. Set OVEN to 350°F for 10 minutes, checking after 8 minutes. Cover and cook until turkey is cooked through. Remove turkey from pot and let stand 5 minutes before slicing.

4. Stir chili sauce and Worcestershire sauce in bowl. Serve chili sauce mixture with turkey.

NINJA SERVING TIP

Substitute chicken or pork tenderloins for turkey if desired.

STOVETOP/SLOW COOK

PORK CARNITAS

Well-browned pork cooks to succulent tenderness in a mixture of onion, garlic, vinegar, and brown sugar. Browning the pork in the pot first gives it a flavorful start.

PREP: 10 minutes • **COOK:** 4 hours, 10 minutes • **SERVINGS:** 10

Ingredients

1 tablespoon olive oil

3 to 4 pounds boneless pork shoulder

1 medium onion, sliced

3 cloves garlic, minced

1 cup chicken broth

¾ cup cider vinegar

2 tablespoons packed brown sugar

2 tablespoons dried oregano leaves, crushed

20 corn tortillas

2 tomatoes, chopped

Directions

1. Pour oil into pot. Set to STOVETOP HIGH and heat oil. Add pork to pot. Cook uncovered 10 minutes until browned on all sides. Add onion and garlic to pot.

2. Stir broth, vinegar, brown sugar, and oregano in bowl. Pour broth mixture over pork in pot. Set to SLOW COOK HIGH for 4 to 5 hours. Cover and cook until pork is fork-tender. Using 2 forks, shred pork in pot.

3. Place **about 1/3 cup** pork mixture on **each** tortilla. Fold tortillas over filling. Sprinkle with tomatoes.

NINJA SERVING TIP

Flavorful enough to be served simply as shown above, you can also add your favorite taco toppings or use pork as a filling for burritos or enchiladas.

STOVETOP/SLOW COOK

MEDITERRANEAN CHICKEN WITH ARTICHOKES & COUSCOUS

Succulent chicken thighs brown in pot to anchor the flavor in this one-pot dish. Couscous cooks in flavorful cooking liquid at the end.

PREP: 15 minutes • **COOK:** 4 hours, 5 minutes • **SERVINGS:** 8

Ingredients

1 tablespoon olive oil

8 bone-in skinless chicken thighs

1 large onion, chopped

4 cloves garlic, chopped

1 can (28 ounces) crushed tomatoes

1 package (8 ounces) frozen artichokes, thawed and drained

1 tablespoon Italian seasoning, crushed

1 teaspoon salt

½ teaspoon ground black pepper

1 cup uncooked couscous

½ cup pitted ripe olives

Directions

1. Pour oil into pot. Set to STOVETOP HIGH and heat oil. Add chicken in batches to pot. Cook uncovered 5 minutes or until chicken is lightly browned.

2. Add onion, garlic, tomatoes, artichokes, Italian seasoning, salt, and black pepper to pot. Set to SLOW COOK HIGH for 4 to 5 hours. Cover and cook, stirring in couscous and olives during last 15 minutes of cooking time.

NINJA SERVING TIP

Sprinkle with toasted pine nuts before serving.

Entrees

 **STOVETOP/OVEN**

VEGETARIAN STUFFED PEPPERS

Peppers stuffed with couscous, chickpeas, and zucchini cook in a chunky tomato-onion sauce. Sauté onion for the sauce, then bake peppers, all in one pot!

PREP: 20 minutes • **COOK:** 35 minutes • **SERVINGS:** 4

Ingredients

2 tablespoons olive oil

1 small onion, chopped

1 can (28 ounces) Italian-style diced tomatoes

1 cup vegetable broth

Salt and ground black pepper

2 cups cooked couscous

1 zucchini, chopped

1 can (about 15 ounces) chickpeas, drained and rinsed

1 tablespoon chopped garlic

1 teaspoon Italian seasoning

½ cup grated Parmesan cheese

4 large red, yellow, or green peppers, tops, seeds, and membranes removed and discarded

Directions

1. Pour oil into pot. Set to STOVETOP MED and heat oil. Stir in onion. Cook uncovered 8 minutes or until onion is tender, stirring occasionally. Stir in tomatoes and broth and season with salt and black pepper.

2. Stir couscous, zucchini, chickpeas, garlic, seasoning, and **half** the cheese in bowl. Season with salt and black pepper. Spoon couscous mixture into peppers and sprinkle with remaining cheese.

3. Place filled peppers into pot. Set OVEN to 250°F for 20 minutes. Cover and cook until peppers are tender.
Serve peppers with tomato sauce.

NINJA HEALTHY TIP

For a healthier version of this, simply omit the cheese.

HONEY ORANGE GLAZED CARROTS • PAGE 90

CHAPTER 6:
Side Dishes

 STEAM OVEN

ASPARAGUS WITH LEMON AIOLI

Asparagus stay beautifully green and fresh-tasting even after cooking to tenderness — the secret is the steam! A lemony garlic sauce highlights its delicate flavor.

PREP: 10 minutes • **COOK:** 10 minutes • **SERVINGS:** 4

Ingredients

1 lemon

⅓ cup light mayonnaise

1 small garlic clove, minced

¼ teaspoon salt

Ground black pepper

1 cup water

1 pound asparagus, trimmed

Directions

1. Grate ½ teaspoon zest and squeeze 2 teaspoons juice from lemon into bowl. Stir in mayonnaise, garlic, and salt. Season with black pepper.

2. Pour water into pot. Place roasting rack into pot. Place asparagus on rack. Set OVEN to 350°F for 10 minutes. Cover and cook until asparagus is tender.

3. Season asparagus with additional salt and black pepper. Serve with lemon aioli.

NINJA TIME-SAVER TIP

Some stores carry pre-trimmed, washed fresh asparagus in the produce section. Try it to save on prep time!

 STOVETOP

BUTTERNUT SQUASH RISOTTO WITH BACON & SAGE

The butternut squash gives this risotto a lovely golden color. It cooks to creamy perfection in the pot with bacon and fresh sage.

PREP: 25 minutes • **COOK:** 1 hour, 5 minutes • **SERVINGS:** 6

Ingredients

1 tablespoon olive oil

2 medium onions, chopped

4 strips bacon, chopped

2 tablespoons chopped fresh sage leaves

1 cup uncooked Arborio rice

½ teaspoon salt

¼ teaspoon ground black pepper

4 cups chicken broth

2 cups peeled and chopped fresh butternut squash

¼ cup grated Parmesan cheese

Directions

1. Pour oil into pot. Set to STOVETOP HIGH and heat oil. Add onions, bacon, and sage to pot. Cook uncovered 10 minutes or until onions are tender, stirring occasionally. Stir rice, salt, and black pepper into pot. Cook uncovered 5 minutes, stirring often. Stir in broth. Cook 10 minutes.

2. Stir squash into pot. Set to STOVETOP LOW. Cover and cook 20 minutes or until rice and squash are tender.

3. Stir cheese into pot. Set to STOVETOP HIGH. Cook uncovered 10 minutes or until liquid is absorbed but mixture is creamy, stirring occasionally.

NINJA SERVING TIP

Serve sprinkled with additional chopped fresh sage leaves, if desired.

⊚ STOVETOP

HONEY ORANGE GLAZED CARROTS

These carrots are so delicious, you will want to make them often — thank goodness they're so quick and easy! Carrot slices cook until tender in a glaze of orange, butter, honey, and thyme.

PREP: 10 minutes • **COOK:** 18 minutes • **SERVINGS:** 6

Ingredients

2 large oranges

1½ pounds carrots, peeled and cut into ½-inch thick slices

2 tablespoons butter

1 teaspoon salt

2 tablespoons honey

1 teaspoon fresh thyme leaves, minced, or ¼ teaspoon dried thyme

Directions

1. Grate ½ **teaspoon** zest and squeeze ¾ **cup** juice from oranges.

2. Stir carrots, **1 tablespoon** butter, orange juice, and salt in pot. Set to STOVETOP HIGH. Cover and cook 10 minutes or until carrots are tender-crisp, stirring occasionally.

3. Uncover pot. Cook uncovered until liquid is reduced to **2 tablespoons**. Stir in remaining butter, honey, orange zest, and thyme. Cook uncovered 3 minutes or until carrots are tender, stirring often.

NINJA SERVING TIP

These are wonderful served with rotisserie chicken breast and coleslaw purchased at the grocery store.

 **OVEN**

CRUSTY, CHEESY POTATOES AU GRATIN

Cream and Gruyère cheese are the stars in this decadent dish. Potatoes absorb the flavors as they cook to tenderness.

PREP: 15 minutes • **COOK:** 1 hour • **SERVINGS:** 4

Ingredients

Cooking spray

1 cup shredded Gruyère or Cheddar cheese (about 4 ounces)

2 large russet potatoes or 4 Yukon Gold potatoes, peeled and thinly sliced

2 tablespoons butter, cut into small pieces

Salt and ground black pepper

Directions

1. Spray 9 x 5 loaf pan with cooking spray.

2. Layer cheese, potatoes, and butter in the pan as follows: **one-fourth** cheese, **one-third** potatoes, **half** butter. Repeat layers, seasoning with salt and black pepper. Top with ¼ cup cheese, then remaining potatoes. Pour cream over potatoes and sprinkle with remaining cheese. Cover pan with foil.

3. Place roasting rack into pot. Place pan on rack. Set OVEN to 375°F for 1 hour. Cover and cook until potatoes are tender.

 SERVING TIP

Serve with grilled steaks and spinach and mushroom salad.

STEAM OVEN/SLOW COOK

GARLICKY MASHED POTATOES

These creamy garlic mashed potatoes not only taste better than your old standby, but they are easier to make, too! The potatoes and garlic cook in the perfect amount of water, so there is no need to drain them before mashing.

PREP: 10 minutes • **COOK:** 30 minutes • **SERVINGS:** 12

Ingredients

5 pounds russet potatoes, peeled and diced

4 cloves garlic, peeled

2 cups water

½ cup butter, cut up

1½ cups hot milk or heavy cream

Salt and ground black pepper

Directions

1. Place potatoes, garlic, and water into pot. Set OVEN to 350°F for 30 minutes. Cover and cook until potatoes are tender. Turn off pot.

2. Mash potatoes with butter and milk. Season with salt and black pepper. Serve immediately or set to SLOW COOK BUFFET for 1 hour or until ready to serve.

NINJA HEALTHY TIP

Substitute chicken broth for milk or cream and reduce amount of butter to save some calories in a lighter version of this recipe. Yukon Gold potatoes can also be substituted for the russets.

 OVEN

EGGPLANT & ARTICHOKE PARMESAN

Enjoy flavors of Eggplant Parmesan without all the work — just assemble and bake! Eggplant and artichokes in a chunky tomato sauce are topped with bread crumbs and melted cheese — delicious!

PREP: 10 minutes • **COOK:** 50 minutes • **SERVINGS:** 6

Ingredients

1 large eggplant (about 1½ pounds), cut in ¾-inch pieces

1 jar (about 24 ounces) marinara sauce

1 can (14.5 ounces) diced tomatoes, undrained

1 can (about 14 ounces) artichoke hearts, rinsed, drained, and quartered

1 small onion, chopped

½ cup Italian-seasoned dry bread crumbs

1 cup shredded mozzarella cheese

½ cup grated Parmesan cheese

Directions

1. Place eggplant, sauce, tomatoes, artichokes, and onion in pot. Set OVEN to 325ºF for 50 minutes. Cover and cook 40 minutes, stirring once halfway through cooking time.

2. Top with bread crumbs and cheeses. Cover and cook 10 minutes or until cheese is melted.

NINJA SERVING TIP

This tastes wonderful topped with ¼ cup toasted pine nuts.

 **STOVETOP/OVEN**

CUBAN BLACK BEANS & RICE

Sautéing the uncooked rice in the pot before adding water heightens the flavor of the finished dish. Mashing some of the beans before adding gives the dish a heartier texture.

PREP: 15 minutes • **COOK:** 40 minutes • **SERVINGS:** 6

Ingredients

1 tablespoon olive oil

1 large onion, chopped

1 large green or red pepper, chopped

4 cloves garlic, minced

1 cup uncooked regular long-grain white rice

1 teaspoon dried oregano, crushed

1 teaspoon ground cumin

¾ teaspoon salt

¼ teaspoon ground black pepper

2 cans (about 15 ounces each) black beans, rinsed and drained

2 cups water

1 can (about 15 ounces) diced tomatoes, undrained

Directions

1. Pour oil into pot. Set to STOVETOP HIGH and heat oil. Add onion and pepper to pot. Cook uncovered 10 minutes or until vegetables are tender-crisp, stirring occasionally. Add garlic to pot. Cook 2 minutes, stirring often. Stir in rice, oregano, cumin, salt, and black pepper. Cook 2 minutes, stirring often.

2. Place **1 cup** beans in bowl and mash coarsely with fork. Stir mashed beans, whole beans, water, and tomatoes in pot. Set OVEN to 350°F for 25 minutes. Cover and cook until liquid is absorbed and rice is tender, stirring occasionally after 15 minutes of cooking time.

 SERVING TIP

Serve sprinkled with chopped fresh cilantro leaves.

REDUCED-FAT NEW YORK-STYLE CHEESECAKE • PAGE 111

CHAPTER 7:
Desserts

Desserts

OVEN

PEACH ALMOND COBBLER WITH COOKIE TOPPING

Frozen peaches make the prep easy in this recipe. The reserved juices thicken in the pot to make a delicious cobbler filling topped with crunchy cookie crumbs.

PREP: 10 minutes • **COOK:** 30 minutes • **SERVINGS:** 8

Ingredients

4 bags (16 ounces each) frozen sliced peaches, thawed and drained, juice reserved

2 tablespoons cornstarch

½ cup sugar

2 teaspoons almond extract

1 package (7 ounces) almond or sugar cookies, crushed (about 2 cups crushed)

Sweetened whipped cream

Directions

1. Stir reserved peach juice and cornstarch in pot. Add peaches, sugar, and almond extract and stir to coat. Set OVEN to 325°F for 30 minutes. Cover and bake until peaches are tender.

2. Turn off pot. Let peach mixture cool in pot 5 minutes. Sprinkle with cookie crumbs. Serve with whipped cream.

NINJA HEALTHY TIP

For a healthful twist, try using your favorite granola or chopped toasted almonds instead of almond cookies.

 **STEAM OVEN**

EASY CRÈME BRÛLÉE

Steam baking takes the place of a traditional water bath in this recipe, yielding velvety-smooth custards topped with caramelized sugar.

PREP: 5 minutes • **COOK:** 1 hour • **CHILL:** 2 hours • **SERVINGS:** 4

Ingredients

1¾ cups heavy cream

⅓ cup plus 4 teaspoons sugar

3 egg yolks

1 teaspoon vanilla extract

2 cups water

Directions

1. Pour heavy cream into microwavable bowl. Microwave on HIGH 3 minutes. Whisk in **1/3 cup** sugar until sugar is dissolved. Slowly whisk **1/3 cup** warm cream into egg yolks in another bowl. Whisk yolk mixture back into remaining cream mixture. Stir in vanilla extract. Pour cream mixture into **4** (6-ounce) ramekins.

2. Pour water into pot. Place roasting rack into pot and place ramekins on rack. Set OVEN to 325°F for 1 hour. Cover with lid and cook until just set. Remove ramekins from pot and let cool. Cover ramekins and refrigerate 2 hours.

3. Remove ramekins from refrigerator and let stand 20 minutes. Sprinkle remaining sugar over custards in ramekins. Use a small cooking torch to caramelize the sugar, forming a candy shell.

NINJA SERVING TIP

If you don't have a torch, you can still serve these custards with a nice, caramelized sugar crust. Heat the broiler during stand time noted above. Sprinkle remaining sugar over custards in ramekins. Place ramekins onto baking sheet. Broil 2 minutes or until sugar is caramelized.

OVEN

IMPOSSIBLE FRENCH APPLE PIE

Apples tossed with cinnamon-sugar bake under a biscuit-like crust, and are sprinkled with a walnut streusel. The pot cooks the apples until soft but keeps the crust tender and light.

PREP: 10 minutes • **COOK:** 55 minutes • **SERVINGS:** 8

Ingredients

2 large Granny Smith apples, peeled, cored, and thinly sliced

⅓ cup granulated sugar

1 teaspoon ground cinnamon

Cooking spray

1⅓ cups all-purpose baking mix

¾ cup milk

2 eggs, beaten

¼ cup butter, softened

¼ cup packed brown sugar

½ cup chopped walnuts

Directions

1. Stir apples, granulated sugar, and cinnamon in bowl. Spray multi-purpose pan with cooking spray. Place apple mixture into pan.

2. Stir **2/3 cup** baking mix, milk, and eggs in bowl. Pour batter over apple mixture.

3. Stir butter, brown sugar, remaining baking mix, and walnuts in bowl. Spoon walnut mixture over batter. Place roasting rack into pot and place multi-purpose pan onto rack. Set OVEN to 400°F for 55 minutes. Cover and cook until top springs back when lightly touched.

 SERVING TIP

Top each serving with frozen vanilla yogurt.

STEAM OVEN/STOVETOP

GLUTEN-FREE CHOCOLATE ALMOND MINI CUPCAKES

Gluten-free never tasted so good. These little gems are fudgy, delicious brownie bites.

PREP: 10 minutes • **COOK:** 20 minutes • **SERVINGS:** 30

Ingredients

3½ tablespoons unsalted butter, melted

1¾ ounces dark or bittersweet chocolate, melted

2 large eggs

¼ cup cane sugar

½ teaspoon gluten-free vanilla extract

2 tablespoons buckwheat flour

2 tablespoons almond flour

2 cups water

2 teaspoons honey

1½ tablespoons water

¼ cup sliced almonds

Directions

1. In a small bowl, combine melted butter and chocolate till blended. With an electric mixer, beat the eggs, sugar, and vanilla on medium speed until pale in color and the batter has doubled in volume. Gently fold in butter and chocolate mixture. Sprinkle the buckwheat flour and almond flour into the batter, and fold gently to combine.

2. Pour the batter into non-stick sprayed silicone mini-muffin tray. Pour 2 cups water into the pot, set the roasting rack in the pot, and the tray on the rack. Set OVEN to 350°F for 15 minutes. Cover and cook 12 minutes or until a toothpick inserted into the center of a cupcake comes out clean.

3. Remove water from pot used for steam baking. Set to STOVETOP HIGH and add honey and 1½ tablespoons water; stir to combine. Add almonds and cook until honey water is concentrated and absorbed in nuts and no liquid remains. Top chocolate cakes with honeyed almonds.

NINJA SERVING TIP

Double the ingredients for the honeyed almonds and use to sprinkle on salads or use as a yogurt mix-in.

 STEAM OVEN

CAPPUCCINO MOLTEN LAVA CAKES

Take the guesswork out of baking molten chocolate cakes. The efficient heating in the pot bakes the outsides to perfection, leaving a gooey chocolate-coffee center.

PREP: 5 minutes • **COOK:** 20 minutes • **SERVINGS:** 6

Ingredients

Cooking spray

1 cup semi-sweet chocolate chips, melted

½ cup butter, melted

1 cup confectioners' sugar

2 eggs

2 egg yolks

2 tablespoons coffee-flavored liqueur

1 teaspoon vanilla extract

½ cup flour

2 cups water

Directions

1. Spray 6-muffin pan cups with cooking spray. Line bottoms of muffin pan cups with waxed paper circles and spray with cooking spray.

2. In a medium bowl, add chocolate and butter and stir until smooth. Stir in sugar. Stir in eggs and egg yolks. Stir in liqueur, vanilla extract, and flour. Spoon batter into muffin pan cups.

3. Pour water into pot. Place roasting rack into pot and muffin cups on rack. Set OVEN to 425°F for 20 minutes. Cover and cook until sides of cakes are firm but centers are still soft. Remove pan from pot and let stand 2 minutes. Run knife around sides of cakes to loosen. Invert onto serving plate. Serve warm.

 SERVING TIP

Serve with whipped cream dusted with cinnamon. Try different flavors by substituting raspberry or hazelnut liqueur for the coffee-flavored liqueur.

STEAM OVEN

LIGHT CARROT CAKE

Not only is this 70-calorie-per-serving dessert flavorful and delicious, but adding carrots and citrus juice will makes it healthy.

PREP: 20 minutes • **COOK:** 35 minutes • **SERVINGS:** 20

Ingredients

¼ pound carrots, peeled and chopped into 1 inch pieces

4¼ cups water

2 eggs

¾ cup sugar

1 teaspoon baking powder

1 teaspoon cinnamon

½ teaspoon ginger

1 cup flour

¼ cup non-fat milk

1 tablespoon butter

1 teaspoon vanilla

Directions

1. Place carrots in a microwave-safe bowl filled with ¼ **cup** water. Steam carrots until soft, about 10 minutes. Using a blender or food processor, purée carrots with remaining cooking liquid until completely smooth. Measure ¼ **cup** and set aside.

2. In an electric mixer, beat the eggs with the sugar on medium speed until thick and pale yellow. In a small bowl, sift together the flour, baking powder, cinnamon, and ginger. Place the milk and butter in a glass measuring cup. Microwave for 40 seconds. Add the ¼ cup of carrot to the milk and butter and set aside. Gradually add flour mixture to egg and sugar mixture on low speed. Gently stir in milk and carrot mixture, then vanilla.

3. Pour batter into non-stick sprayed loaf pan. Pour remaining water into the pot, and place the loaf pan on rack in pot. Set OVEN to 325°F for 35 minutes, checking for doneness after 30 minutes. Cover and cook until a toothpick stuck into the center of the cake comes out clean.

NUTRITION PER SERVING:
70 CALORIES; 1G FAT; 0.5G
SATURATED FAT; 35MG SODIUM;
14G CARBOHYDRATE; 0G FIBER;
1G PROTEIN

NINJA SERVING TIP

Combine 1 teaspoon each of lemon juice and orange juice. Add 1/8 teaspoon of ground ginger to form a glaze. Drizzle on cake as desired.

LIGHT CHOCOLATE LOAF WITH HAZELNUT PRALINE

This cake is light and airy and with only 99 calories per slice, it makes a delicious treat any time of day.

PREP: 15 minutes • **COOK:** 30 minutes • **SERVINGS:** 20

Ingredients

2 eggs

¾ cup sugar plus ⅓ cup sugar

1 cup flour

1 teaspoon baking powder

½ teaspoon salt

¼ cup bittersweet chocolate, melted

1 tablespoon butter, melted

½ cup skim milk

Cooking spray

2¼ cups water

½ cup chopped toasted hazelnuts

Directions

1. In an electric mixer, beat the eggs with **¾ cup** sugar on medium speed until thick and pale yellow, about 10 minutes.

2. In a small bowl, sift together the flour, baking powder, and salt. In another small bowl, mix together melted chocolate and butter. Add the milk to the melted chocolate and butter mixture and set aside.

3. Gradually add flour mixture to egg and sugar mixture on low speed. Gently stir in chocolate mixture. Spray loaf pan with nonstick cooking spray and pour in batter. Add 2 cups water to the pot, place the roasting rack in the pot, and set the loaf pan on the rack. Set OVEN to 325°F for 25 minutes. Cover and cook until a toothpick stuck into the center of the cake comes out clean.

4. Clean pot. Set to STOVETOP MED and add ⅓ cup sugar and ¼ cup water; stir continuously until sugar melts and becomes a caramel. Add the hazelnuts and stir to coat. Spoon hot praline mixture over cake and let cool.

NUTRITION PER SERVING: 99 CALORIES; 4G FAT; 1G SATURATED FAT; 97MG SODIUM; 17G CARBOHYDRATE; 0G FIBER; 2G PROTEIN.

NINJA HEALTHY TIP

This loaf cake is light in calories. Great for a breakfast, each slice is only 99 calories.

STEAM OVEN

LIGHT PUMPKIN SPICE CAKE

This 65-calorie-per-serving cake is great for breakfast or dessert, perfect for fall or winter holiday entertaining. Try roasting your own fresh sugar pumpkin and puréeing the pulp in the fall.

PREP: 10 minutes • **COOK:** 30 minutes • **SERVINGS:** 20

Ingredients

2 eggs

¾ cup sugar

1 cup flour

1 teaspoon baking powder

1 teaspoon cinnamon

½ teaspoon ginger

4 tablespoons non-fat milk

1 tablespoon butter

4 teaspoons pumpkin purée

1 teaspoon vanilla

4 cups water

Directions

1. In an electric mixer, beat the eggs with the sugar on medium speed until thick and pale yellow. In a small bowl, sift together the flour, baking powder, cinnamon, and ginger.

2. In the meantime, place the milk and butter in a glass measuring cup. Microwave for 40 seconds. Add the pumpkin to milk and butter mixture and set aside. Gradually add flour mixture to egg and sugar mixture on low speed. Gently stir in milk and pumpkin mixture, then vanilla.

3. Pour batter into a sprayed non-stick 9 x 5 loaf pan. Pour water into the pot. Place roasting rack in pot and loaf pan on rack. Set OVEN to 325°F for 35 minutes, checking for doneness after 30 minutes. Cover and cook until a toothpick stuck into the center of the cake comes out clean.

NUTRITION PER SERVING: 65 CALORIES; 1G FAT; 0.5G SATURATED FAT; 30MG SODIUM; 13G CARBOHYDRATE; 0G FIBER; 1G PROTEIN

NINJA SERVING TIP

Combine 4 ounces low-fat cream cheese with 1½ teaspoons sugar and ½ teaspoon vanilla for a quick and easy frosting.

 **STEAM OVEN**

LIGHT MINI CUPCAKES

Turn your favorite store-bought cake mix into light, moist, and delicious cupcakes with half the fat, less calories and half the hassle! This recipe is perfect for gluten-free cake mixes, too.

PREP: 5 minutes • **COOK:** 15 minutes • **SERVINGS:** 60

Ingredients

1 box cake mix – 18.25 oz.
(ingredients directed on the box)

Cooking spray

2 cups water

Directions

1. Prepare cake mix with ingredients as directed on box, but reduce fat (butter or oil) by **HALF**. Place 1 tablespoon of batter into each cup of a lightly sprayed 12-cup silicone muffin tray.

2. Pour water into pot. Set roasting rack in pot and place muffin tray on rack.

3. Set OVEN to the highest cooking temperature recommended on box, for 15 minutes, checking after 10 minutes (the additional batches will each take about 5 minutes less time). Cover and cook until a toothpick inserted in center comes out clean.

4. Serve with desired frosting or top with fresh fruit.

 SERVING TIP

Two easy and delicious frostings are lightly sweetened whipped cream or a simple glaze made with 1 cup powdered sugar and 4 teaspoons citrus juice. Top with fresh fruit as desired.

⬛ **STEAM OVEN**

Signature

LIGHT KIWI LIME ANGEL FOOD CUPCAKES

These fun desserts are only 15 calories each! Because they cook so quickly, it is an easy and guilt-free pleasure to whip up for family and friends.

PREP: 10 minutes • **COOK:** 15 minutes • **SERVINGS:** 30

Ingredients

¼ cup cake flour (or all-purpose flour), sifted

3 tablespoons sugar

3 egg whites

¼ teaspoon vanilla extract

Pinch salt

¼ teaspoon cream of tartar

2 teaspoons lime zest

3 teaspoons lime juice

2 cups water

4 tablespoons powdered sugar

1 kiwi, peeled, thinly sliced, and cut into quarters (pie-shaped)

Directions

1. In a small bowl, combine cake flour with **1 tablespoon** sugar.

2. With an electric mixer set to high, beat egg whites, vanilla extract, salt, and cream of tartar until soft peaks form. Add **1 teaspoon** lime zest and **1 teaspoon** lime juice. Gradually add remaining 2 tablespoons sugar. Beat on high until mixture is fully incorporated, glossy, and stiff peaks are formed.

3. Fold in by hand flour and sugar mixture in thirds until fully incorporated, keeping batter as voluminous as possible.

4. Fill silicone mini-muffin tray with 1 tablespoon batter in each cup. Pour water into pot. Place roasting rack in pot and tray on rack. Set OVEN to 325°F for 15 minutes, checking after 12 minutes, and cook until cupcakes rise and a toothpick inserted in centers comes out clean. Remove mini cupcakes and let cool.

5. Stir together remaining lime zest, 2 teaspoons lime juice, and powdered sugar and frost the tops of the cakes. Top with kiwi.

NUTRITION PER SERVING: 15 CALORIES; 0G FAT; 0G SATURATED FAT; 10MG SODIUM; 4G CARBOHYDRATE; 0G FIBER; 0G PROTEIN

NINJA SERVING TIP

Cake flour will create a delicate, tender crumb, but all-purpose flour will work if that is what you have.

STEAM OVEN

Signature

LIGHT MINI STRAWBERRY SHORTCAKES

Finding farm stands selling local in-season berries is worth the drive. Buy extra and freeze some for winter smoothies. This recipe is also low on calories at only 40 each.

PREP: 10 minutes • **COOK:** 15 minutes • **SERVINGS:** 30

Ingredients

1 egg

⅓ cup sugar plus 1½ teaspoons sugar

½ cup flour

½ teaspoon baking powder

¼ cup skim milk

½ tablespoon butter, melted

½ teaspoon vanilla

2 cups water

½ cup heavy cream

15 strawberries, hulled and sliced ¼ inch

Directions

1. With an electric mixer, beat the egg with **1/3 cup** sugar on medium speed until thick and pale yellow, about 5 to 10 minutes. In a small bowl, sift together the flour and baking powder. In another bowl, stir together milk and butter; set aside.

2. Gradually add flour mixture to egg and sugar mixture on low speed. Gently stir in milk and butter mixture, then vanilla. Scoop 1 tablespoon of batter into each cup of a silicone mini-muffin tray.

3. Pour water into pot. Place rack in pot and mini-muffin tray on rack. Set OVEN to 325°F for 15 minutes, cover and cook, checking after 10 minutes or until a toothpick stuck into the center of a cupcake comes out clean; let cool.

4. Beat heavy cream and 1½ teaspoons of sugar together until peaks form. Top mini cupcakes with whipped cream and a slice of strawberry.

NUTRITION PER SERVING:
40 CALORIES; 2G FAT; 1G
SATURATED FAT; 10MG SODIUM;
5G CARBOHYDRATE; 0G FIBER;
0G PROTEIN

NINJA SERVING TIP

Swap out the strawberry with any fresh fruit that is ripe or in season as desired.

REDUCED-FAT NEW YORK-STYLE CHEESECAKE

This cheesecake is best removed from the oven when there is still a bit of jiggle left to the cake. The cheesecake will firm up in the refrigerator and maintain a perfect creamy consistency.

PREP: 15 minutes • **COOK:** 55 minutes • **SERVINGS:** 10

Ingredients

Cooking spray

½ cup plus 2 tablespoons graham cracker crumbs

2 tablespoons margarine, melted

¼ cup plus 3 tablespoons sugar

12 ounces Neufchâtel cream cheese (1½ packages), softened

1 teaspoon vanilla

1 egg

1 egg white

½ cup fat-free sour cream

4 cups water

¾ cup fresh raspberries

Directions

1. Spray bottom of 6-inch round cake pan with cooking spray. Combine graham cracker crumbs, margarine, and **1 tablespoon** sugar. Press evenly into pan.

2. Beat cream cheese, remaining sugar, and vanilla in a large bowl with electric mixer on medium speed until well blended. Beat in eggs and egg whites till well blended. Add sour cream; mix well. Pour into prepared pan. Pour water in bottom of pot, place rack in pot and cheesecake pan on rack, and cover with lid. Set OVEN to 325°F for 55 minutes, checking after 50 minutes for doneness. Cover and cook until center is almost set. Remove cake to a rack and let cool completely.

3. Refrigerate 4 hours or overnight. To remove from pan (if a non-spring-form pan), rest cheesecake pan in a pan with very warm water for about 2 minutes. Run a knife around the edges of the pan to loosen cheesecake, invert pan upside-down on a plate, and gently tap on bottom of pan to loosen. Top with raspberries just before serving.

NUTRITION PER SERVING: 190 CALORIES; 11G FAT; 5G SATURATED FAT; 210MG SODIUM; 18G CARBOHYDRATE; 1G FIBER; 5G PROTEIN

NINJA SERVING TIP

Serve topped with fresh fruit (sliced strawberries, blueberries or raspberries), fruit preserves, lemon curd, caramel sauce, toasted chopped pecans, or mini chocolate chips.

BAKED BREAKFAST OATMEAL • PAGE 116

CHAPTER 8:
Breakfasts

 STEAM OVEN

BLUEBERRY PANCAKE MUFFINS

Buttermilk blueberry pancakes — in a muffin! These
quick-to-make muffins bake up light and moist in the pot,
thanks to the steam-baking technique.

PREP: 15 minutes • **COOK:** 25 minutes • **SERVINGS:** 6

Ingredients

1 cup all-purpose flour

1½ teaspoons baking powder

¼ teaspoon baking soda

¼ teaspoon salt

2 teaspoons sugar

¾ cup buttermilk

1 tablespoon canola oil

1 egg

**3 tablespoons canned blueberries,
  drained**

Cooking spray

1½ cups hot water

Directions

1. Stir flour, baking powder, baking soda, salt, and sugar in a bowl.

2. Beat buttermilk, oil, and egg in another bowl. Add buttermilk mixture to flour mixture and stir just until combined. Stir in blueberries.

3. Spray 6-cup muffin pan with cooking spray. Spoon batter into muffin-pan cups.

4. Pour water into pot. Place roasting rack into pot. Place pan on rack. Set OVEN to 350°F for 25 minutes. Cover and cook until wooden pick inserted in centers comes out clean.

NINJA SERVING TIP

Sprinkle with confectioners' sugar and serve with maple butter.

STOVETOP/SLOW COOK

BAKED BREAKFAST OATMEAL

Hearty steel-cut oats cook until tender in a mixture of hot milk, maple syrup, butter, vanilla, and spices. No need to stir; the mixture slow cooks perfectly. Sweet, tart dried cherries are the perfect finish.

PREP: 15 minutes • **COOK:** 2 hours, 10 minutes • **SERVINGS:** 4

Ingredients

4 cups milk

4 tablespoons pure maple syrup

2 tablespoons butter, cut up

2 teaspoons vanilla extract

1 teaspoon ground cinnamon

¼ teaspoon ground nutmeg

Pinch salt

1 cup uncooked steel-cut oats

1 cup dried cherries

Directions

1. Stir milk, syrup, butter, vanilla extract, cinnamon, nutmeg, and salt in pot. Set to STOVETOP HIGH. Cover and cook 10 minutes or until butter is melted.

2. Stir in oats. Set to SLOW COOK HIGH for 2 to 3 hours. Cover and cook until oats are tender and mixture is creamy. Stir in cherries.

NINJA SERVING TIP

Try adding cut-up bananas, apples, pears, or raisins. For creamier oatmeal, stir in a touch of milk with each serving.

STOVETOP/SLOW COOK

APPLE FRENCH TOAST CASSEROLE

This warm bread pudding is perfect for a special breakfast or brunch. Apples and pecans cook in the pot with a maple-butter sauce, then are tossed with cubes of challah bread in a spiced milk mixture. Cover and let the sweet aroma fill your kitchen as it cooks.

PREP: 20 minutes • **COOK:** 2 hours, 10 minutes • **SERVINGS:** 6

Ingredients

½ **cup butter**

2 **Granny Smith apples, peeled, cored, and chopped**

1 **cup chopped pecans**

½ **cup packed brown sugar**

½ **cup pure maple syrup**

1 **loaf challah bread (about 1 pound), cut into cubes**

6 **large eggs**

2 **cups milk**

2 **teaspoons ground cinnamon**

1 **tablespoon vanilla extract**

Pinch salt

Confectioners' sugar

Directions

1. Place butter into pot. Set to STOVETOP HIGH and heat until butter is melted. Place apples, pecans, brown sugar, and syrup in pot. Cook uncovered 10 minutes, stirring often or until apples are tender.

2. Place bread in bowl. Beat eggs, milk, cinnamon, vanilla extract, and salt in another bowl. Pour egg mixture over bread and stir to coat. Pour bread mixture into pot and stir. Set to SLOW COOK HIGH for 2 to 3 hours. Cover and cook until center is set. Turn off pot. Let stand 10 minutes before serving. Sprinkle with confectioners' sugar.

NINJA HEALTHY TIP

Use refrigerated egg substitute in place of eggs and 1% milk instead of whole as a healthier swap of ingredients.

 STOVETOP

FRITTATA WITH HASH BROWN POTATOES & BACON

This Italian omelet is loaded with peppers, potatoes, bacon, and cheese. Cook everything in the pot — then stir in the eggs and cover to finish cooking — the frittata stays moist and delicious.

PREP: 15 minutes • **COOK:** 30 minutes • **SERVINGS:** 6

Ingredients

2 tablespoons canola oil

1 large onion, chopped

1 large green pepper, chopped

4 strips bacon, chopped

½ of a 32-ounce package frozen diced hash brown potatoes (about 3½ cups)

12 eggs

¾ cup milk

½ teaspoon salt

¼ teaspoon ground black pepper

1 cup shredded Cheddar cheese

Directions

1. Pour oil into pot. Set to STOVETOP HIGH and heat oil. Add onion, green pepper, and bacon to pot. Cook uncovered 15 minutes, stirring often or until vegetables are tender.

2. Stir in potatoes. Cover and cook 5 minutes.

3. Beat eggs, milk, salt, and black pepper in bowl. Set pot to STOVETOP MED. Stir egg mixture and cheese into pot. Cover and cook 10 minutes or until the egg mixture is set.

NINJA SERVING TIP

Serve topped with additional chopped cooked bacon, if desired.

STOVETOP/OVEN

CARAMELIZED ONION FRITTATA

The steady heat in the pot allows the sugars in the onions to caramelize without scorching, resulting in deeply browned onions with spectacular flavor. Stir in the eggs and Gruyère cheese and bake to make a perfect Italian omelet!

PREP: 10 minutes • **COOK:** 30 minutes • **SERVINGS:** 8

Ingredients

12 eggs

Salt and ground black pepper

2 tablespoons butter

1 tablespoon canola oil

4 onions, thinly sliced

1 tablespoon chopped fresh thyme leaves

1½ cups grated Gruyère cheese

Chopped fresh chives

Directions

1. Beat eggs in bowl. Season with salt and black pepper.

2. Place butter and oil into pot. Set to STOVETOP HIGH and heat until butter is melted. Add onions and thyme to pot and season with salt and black pepper. Cook uncovered 20 minutes or until onions are deep brown and tender, stirring occasionally.

3. Stir eggs in pot. Cook 1 minute. Stir in cheese. Set OVEN to 325°F for 10 minutes, checking after 7 minutes. Cover and cook until egg mixture is set, stirring once halfway through cooking time.

4. Invert frittata onto serving platter. Sprinkle with chives.

NINJA SERVING TIP

Butter a slice of toasted Italian bread and place a frittata square in the middle for the perfect Italian egg sandwich.

STEAM OVEN

LOW-FAT SPICED MAPLE CORN MUFFINS

Start with a box of packaged corn muffin mix, then spice it up with maple syrup and cinnamon for a new favorite breakfast treat. The pot insulates as it bakes, which means that your corn muffins are always moist.

PREP: 5 minutes • **COOK:** 15 minutes • **SERVINGS:** 6

Ingredients

Cooking spray

1 package (6.5 ounces) cornbread and muffin mix

2 egg whites

¼ cup fat-free milk

¼ cup pure maple syrup

1 teaspoon ground cinnamon

2 cups water

Directions

1. Spray 6-cup muffin pan with cooking spray.

2. Stir muffin mix, egg whites, milk, syrup, and cinnamon in bowl. Spoon batter into muffin-pan cups.

3. Pour water into pot. Place roasting rack into pot. Place pan onto rack. Set OVEN to 400°F for 15 minutes. Cover and bake until wooden pick inserted in centers comes out clean.

 **NINJA** SERVING TIP

Serve with your favorite fruit butter, like apple butter or pumpkin butter.

STOVETOP/SLOW COOK

TURKEY SAUSAGE, EGG, & CHEESE STRATA

This one-pot breakfast features eggs, sausage, tomatoes, cheese, and bread for a hearty start to your day and is especially great for weekend brunch.

PREP: 20 minutes • **COOK:** 2 hours, 20 minutes • **SERVINGS:** 6

Ingredients

1 tablespoon canola oil

1¼ pounds turkey sausage, casing removed

1 medium onion, chopped

1 tablespoon chopped garlic

2 medium plum tomatoes, chopped

1 tablespoon dried basil leaves, crushed

10 eggs, beaten

2 cups milk

5 cups sliced Italian bread cut into ½-inch pieces

1 cup shredded Monterey Jack cheese

Salt and ground black pepper

Directions

1. Pour oil into pot. Set to STOVETOP HIGH and heat oil. Add sausage to pot. Cook uncovered 10 minutes or until sausage is cooked through, stirring occasionally. Remove sausage from pot.

2. Stir onion, garlic, tomatoes, and basil in pot. Cook uncovered 5 minutes or until onion is tender, stirring occasionally. Remove vegetable mixture from pot.

3. Stir eggs, milk, bread, cheese, salt, and black pepper in bowl. Stir in sausage and vegetable mixture. Pour egg mixture into pot. Set to SLOW COOK HIGH for 2 to 3 hours. Cover and cook until mixture is set.

NINJA SERVING TIP

For a spicy dish, use hot Italian sausage instead of turkey sausage.

 **STOVETOP/OVEN**

BACON, EGG, & CHEESE CASSEROLE WITH SPINACH

Breakfast favorites bake together in this fantastic casserole. Cook bacon until crisp; add bread, eggs, cheese, and spinach; and bake, all right in the pot. Simple and delicious.

PREP: 10 minutes • **COOK:** 40 minutes • **SERVINGS:** 6

Ingredients

4 slices bacon, chopped

8 eggs

2½ cups half and half

1 cup shredded Cheddar cheese

½ cup shredded Parmesan cheese

¼ teaspoon ground black pepper

4 slices multi-grain or whole wheat bread, crusts removed, and cut into 1-inch cubes

4 cups fresh baby spinach, coarsely chopped

Directions

1. Add bacon to pot. Set to STOVETOP HIGH. Cook uncovered 10 minutes or until bacon is crisp, stirring occasionally. Remove bacon from pot and drain on paper towels. Spoon off fat.

2. Beat eggs, half and half, cheeses, and black pepper in bowl. Put bread, spinach, and bacon in pot. Stir in egg mixture. Set OVEN to 300°F for 30 minutes. Cover and cook until mixture is set. Turn off pot and let stand 10 minutes before serving.

 **SERVING TIP**

This casserole makes a great brunch dish or light supper. Serve with a green salad.

CHAPTER 9:
Charts & Index

Steam-Infused Roasting

		Cooking Infusions		
Protein	Flavor Choice	Liquid	Seasoning	Extra Flavor Ingredients
CHICKEN *1 hour cooktime for 3-4 lbs.* *Steam Oven at 375°F*	Tuscan	3 cups White Wine, ½ cup Lemon Juice	1 cup Arugula	1 cup Fennel, 1 cup Pear
	Mediterranean	4 cups Chicken Broth	2 teaspoons dried Oregano	½ cup Feta Cheese
	Caribbean	2 cups Orange Juice, 2 cups Broth	1 cup Onion, 2 cups Bell Pepper	2 tablespoons Cumin, 1 cup Cilantro
	Thai	2 cans Coconut Milk, ½ cup Water	1½ tablespoons minced Ginger	¼ cup Curry Paste
FISH *30 minutes cooktime for 2 lbs.* *Steam Oven at 350°F*	Southern	2 cups Fish Stock	½ cup Onion	½ cup Bacon, 1 cup Corn
	French	2 cups White Wine	1 cup Leek	1 cup Mushrooms
	Italian	2 cups Broth	2 teaspoons dried Basil, 2 minced Garlic Cloves	1 can Cannellini Beans undrained, ½ pkg. frozen Spinach
	Lemon Dill	1½ cups Wine, ½ cup Lemon Juice	1 tablespoon chopped Dill	1 tablespoon Dijon Mustard
PORK *40 minutes cooktime for 2-3 lbs.* *Steam Oven at 375°F*	German	4 cups Chicken Broth	2 minced cloves Garlic, 1 teaspoon Allspice	2 cups Onion
	Sweet/Savory	4 cups Apple Juice	1 cup Onion	4 cups Red Cabbage
	American	2 cups Broth, 2 cups Barbecue Sauce	2 minced Garlic Cloves	½ cup Bacon
	French	4 cups Chicken Broth	4 Cloves	¼ cup Honey Mustard
BEEF *40 minutes cooktime for 2-3 lbs.* *Steam Oven at 350°F*	Mexican	2 cups Salsa, 2 cups Beef Broth	2 tablespoons chopped Chilies, 2 teaspoons Cumin	2 minced Garlic Cloves, ½ cup Cilantro
	Asian	2 cups Teriyaki Sauce, 2 cups Water	½ cup Green Onions, 4 minced Garlic Cloves	½ tablespoon minced Ginger, 2 tablespoons Hot Garlic Paste
	Greek	3 cups Red Wine, 1 cup Water	1 can Tomato Paste, 2 tablespoons Olive Oil	2 tablespoons chopped Rosemary
	Spain	1 can diced Tomatoes, 2 cups Chicken Broth	2 cups Red Bell Pepper, 4 minced Garlic Cloves	1 cup Sherry, 2 teaspoons Saffron

Steam Roast Flavor Substitutes

Have fun with the recipes and take something from ordinary to extraordinary with the quick change of a rub, sauce, flavorful infusion, crispy crust, or warm topping. Try out some of the recommendations below to change up one of your favorites or create a new one!

Flavor Substitutes			
Rubs	Sauces & Glazes	Crispy Crust	Hot Warm Crust
Whether you are Sear/ Cooking, Steam or Oven Roasting, these rubs will definitely kick your meal up a notch.	Baste your meat or fish with these sauces for an extra kick 15–30 minutes before they are done cooking when using your Roast mode.	Pre-crisp in the STOVETOP HIGH setting till golden brown, then just sprinkle over cooked meats, fish, or vegetables.	Place on meat or vegetables 5 minutes before cooking is done.
Lemon Pepper Seasoning	Barbecue Sauce	Ritz, Butter, Parsley	Blue Cheese, Honey
Cajun Seasoning	Southwest Barbecue (blended with Chipotle in Adobo Purée, cumin, and lime juice)	Panko, Butter, Italian Seasoning, Parmesan	Gorgonzola, Walnut
Montreal Seasoning		Panko, Hazelnut, Butter,	Fontina, Garlic, Sautéed Spinach
Peppercorn	Korean Barbecue	Salt, Pepper	Country Dijon Herb
Asian Five Spice Seasoning and Orange Peel	Hoisin	Sesame (Black and White)	Pesto
Garlic, Parsley, Parmesan	Sweet Chili Sauce	Almond, Parsley, Lemon Peel	
Dijon Herb (Try Parsley, Herbs de Provence, or Rosemary)		Zatar, Pistachio	
		Coconut, Macadamia Nut	
		Panko, Coconut, Cayenne	

Slow Cooker Cooking Guide

Beef		
Type of Beef	Cook Time LOW	Cook Time HIGH
Top Round	8–10 hours	4–5 hours
Bottom Round	8–10 hours	4–5 hours
Chuck	8–10 hours	4–5 hours
Stew Meat (Beef, Lamb, Veal, Rabbit)	7–9 hours	3–4 hours
Eye of the Round, Sirloin	6–8 hours	3–4 hours
Short Ribs	7–9 hours	3½–4½ hours
Brisket	7–9 hours	3½–4½ hours
Pot Roast	7–9 hours	3½–4½ hours
Frozen Meatballs (precooked)	6–8 hours	3–4 hours

Pork		
Type of Pork	Cook Time LOW	Cook Time HIGH
Baby Back Ribs	7–9 hours	3½–4½ hours
Country Ribs	7–9 hours	3½–4½ hours
Pork Tenderloin	6–7 hours	3–4 hours
Pork Loin	7–9 hours	3½–4½ hours
Pork Rib Roast	7–9 hours	3½–4½ hours
Pork Butt	10–12 hours	5–6 hours
Pork Shoulder	10–12 hours	5–6 hours
Ham (fully cooked)	5–7 hours	2½–3½ hours
Ham, Bone-In (uncooked)	7–9 hours	3½–4½ hours

Slow Cooker Cooking Guide

Poultry		
Type of Poultry	Cook Time LOW	Cook Time HIGH
Boneless, Skinless Breast	6–7 hours	3–4 hours
Boneless, Skinless Thighs	6–7½ hours	3–4½ hours
Bone-In Breast	6–7½ hours	3–4½ hours
Bone-In Thighs	7–9 hours	3½–4½ hours
Whole Chicken	7–9 hours	3½–4½ hours
Chicken Wings	6–7 hours	3–4 hours
Turkey Breast	7–9 hours	3½–4½ hours
Turkey Thighs	7–9 hours	3½–4½ hours

Fish		
Type of Fish	Cook Time LOW	Cook Time HIGH
1-inch Fillets	---	30–45 minutes
Frozen Shrimp	Add during last 20–30 minutes of cooking	Add during last 20–30 minutes of cooking
Fresh Shellfish	Add during last 20–30 minutes of cooking	Add during last 20–30 minutes of cooking

Layered Meals

Prepare complete meals in a single pot on the OVEN setting by choosing a protein, a vegetable, and a starch from the chart below and layering them in the pot to cook together at the same time. Thicker protein and vegetables will require slightly longer cook times; adjust times as necessary. Layered Meal Instructions: Pre-heat OVEN to 350°F and layer starch on the bottom of the pot with recommended amount of water per the package cooking instructions. Insert the rack and lay protein and vegetables on rack. Close lid and bake according to chart below.

Quick Cooking (9 Minutes or Less)

Protein	Vegetable	Starch
Fish Fillets Small Chicken Cutlets Frozen Shrimp/Frozen Fish Fillets	Thin Asparagus and Thin Zucchini Bell Peppers Haricots Vert Spinach Onions and Mushrooms Pea Pods or Sugar Snap Peas Frozen Peas	Couscous 90-Second Microwave Rice Israeli Couscous Kasha 5-Minute Long Grain Wild Rice

Medium Cooking (10–20 Minutes)

Protein	Vegetable	Starch
Frozen Large Chicken Cutlets Frozen Shrimp/Frozen Fish Fillets	Broccoli Cauliflower Green Beans Thick Asparagus Thick-Sliced Zucchini or Eggplant	10-Minute Quick Barley Farro Bulger Quinoa 10-Minute Rice

Longer Cooking (20+ Minutes)

Protein	Vegetable	Starch
Frozen Boneless Chicken Breast Beef Roast (1½ inch or smaller if using steaming tray) Bone-In Meats, Chicken Thighs	Carrots Sweet Potatoes Parsnips or Turnips Rutabagas Artichokes Corn on the Cob	White Rice Jasmine Rice Pilaf

Seasonal Fruit & Vegetable Guide

	Spring MID MAR – MID JUN	Summer MID JUN – MID SEP	Fall MID SEP – MID DEC	Winter MID DEC – MID MAR
FRUITS	Grapes Honeydew Mangos Papayas Peaches Plums Raspberries Strawberries	Blackberries Blueberries Cantaloupe Cherries Figs Nectarines Strawberries Raspberries Watermelon Wild Blueberries	Apples Asian Pears Cranberries Kiwis Oranges Pineapples	Bananas Clementines Grapefruits Key Limes Lemons Meyer Lemons Minneolas Tangerines
VEGETABLES	Asparagus Avocados Basil Beans Beets Broccoli Cabbage Chile Peppers Chinese Cabbage Chives Cucumbers Iceberg Lettuce Mushrooms Okra Peas Radishes Rhubarb Shallots Spinach Summer Squash Sweet Potatoes Turnips	Basil Beans Beets Chanterelle Mushrooms Cilantro Corn Cucumbers Dates Mint Okra Oregano Rosemary Sweet Peppers Summer Squash Tomatoes Zucchini	Broccoli Brussel Sprouts Cabbage Cauliflower Chicory Chinese Cabbage Cucumbers Dates Fennel Greens Leaf Lettuce Nuts Okra Sage Shallots Spinach Thyme Star Fruit Sweet Potatoes Winter Squash	Avocados Broccoli Brussel Sprouts Cabbage Cauliflower Celery Root Chicory Chinese Cabbage Fennel Greens Spinach Sweet Potatoes

Healthy Substitutions

Use this guide to see how you can make simple ingredient substitutions that will give your recipes a healthy boost.

Healthy Swaps		
	Instead Of	**Substitute This**
DAIRY	Milk, evaporated	Evaporated skim milk
	Whole milk	Fat-free milk
	Cheddar cheese	Low-fat cheddar cheese
	Ice cream	Frozen yogurt or sorbet
	Cream cheese	Neufchâtel or light cream cheese
	Whipped cream	Light whipped topping
	Ricotta cheese	Low-fat ricotta cheese
	Cream	Fat-free half-and-half, evaporated skim milk
	Yogurt, fruit-flavored	Plain low-fat yogurt with fresh fruit slices
	Sour cream, full-fat	Fat-free or low-fat sour cream, plain fat-free or low-fat yogurt
PROTEIN	Bacon	Canadian bacon, turkey bacon, smoked turkey, or lean prosciutto (Italian ham)
	Ground beef	Extra-lean or lean ground beef, skinless chicken or turkey breast, tofu, tempeh
	Meat as the main ingredient	Three times as many vegetables as the meat on pizzas or in casseroles, soups, and stews
	Eggs	Two egg whites or ¼ cup egg substitute for each whole egg
OTHER	Soups, creamed	Fat-free milk-based soups, mashed potato flakes, or puréed carrots, potatoes, or tofu for thickening agents
	Soups, sauces, dressings, crackers, or canned meat, fish, or vegetables	Low-sodium or reduced-sodium versions

Healthy Substitutions

Use this guide to see how you can make simple ingredient substitutions that will give your recipes a healthy boost.

	Healthy Swaps	
	Instead Of	**Substitute This**
GRAINS	Bread, white	Whole-grain bread
	Bread crumbs, dry	Rolled oats or crushed bran cereal
	Pasta, enriched (white)	Whole wheat pasta
	Rice, white	Brown rice, wild rice, bulgur, or pearl barley
FAT	Butter, margarine, shortening, or oil in baked goods	Applesauce or prune purée for half of the called-for butter, shortening, or oil; butter spreads or shortenings specially formulated for baking that don't have trans fats (Note: To avoid dense, soggy, or flat baked goods, don't substitute oil for butter or shortening. Also don't substitute diet, whipped, or tub-style margarine for regular margarine.)
	Butter, margarine, shortening, or oil to prevent sticking	Cooking spray or nonstick pans
	Mayonnaise	Reduced-calorie mayonnaise-type salad dressing or reduced-calorie, reduced-fat mayonnaise
	Oil-based marinades	Wine, balsamic vinegar, fruit juice, or fat-free broth
SUGAR	Sugar	In most baked goods you can reduce the amount of sugar by one-half; intensify sweetness by adding vanilla, nutmeg, or cinnamon.
	Syrup	Puréed fruit, such as applesauce, or low-calorie, sugar-free syrup
	Chocolate chips	Craisins
SAUCES	Soy sauce	Sweet-and-sour sauce, hot mustard sauce, or low-sodium soy sauce
SALT	Salt	Herbs, spices, citrus juices (lemon, lime, orange), rice vinegar, salt-free seasoning mixes or herb blends, low-sodium soy sauce
	Seasoning salt, such as garlic salt, celery salt, or onion salt	Herb-only seasonings, such as garlic powder, celery seed, or onion flakes, or finely chopped herbs or garlic, celery, or onions

Pasta Cooking Chart–No Need to Drain!

For quick and easy pasta preparation that is ready in a snap without the time needed to boil and drain, look no further than your Ninja 3-in-1 Cooking System.

Simply follow the chart below, referring to the recommended cooking time on the box of the pasta. Find the cook time and amount of water needed to cook perfectly done pasta with no draining necessary.

Follow these directions:

Add the pasta, designated amount of water, 1-2 tablespoons butter, and 1 teaspoon of salt to the pot and gently stir to submerge pasta. Set OVEN to 250°F and set timer according to the chart below. Cook covered for 10 minutes, open, stir, cover, and cook for remaining time.

Pasta Cooking Chart			
1 Pound Box Recommended Cook Time	Water	Ninja Cook Time	Percentage of Time Saved with the Ninja*
4 minutes	2¾ cups	10–12 minutes	50% time savings
7 minutes	3 cups	15–18 minutes	33% time savings
9 minutes	3¼ cups	20–22 minutes	31% time savings
11 minutes	3½ cups	20–22 minutes	29% time savings

* Time to boil water (approximately 20 minutes) plus pasta cooking time.

Equivalents Charts

Weight Measurements

USA/UK	Metric
1 oz.	30 g
2 oz.	60 g
3 oz.	90 g
4 oz. (1¼ lb.)	125 g
5 oz. (⅓ lb.)	155 g
6 oz.	185 g
7 oz.	220 g
8 oz. (½ lb.)	125 g
10 oz.	315 g
12 oz. (¾ lb.)	375 g
14 oz.	440 g
16 oz.	500 g
1½ lb.	750 g
2 lb.	1 kg
3 lb.	1½ kg

Length Measurements

⅛ in.	3 mm
¼ in.	6 mm
½ in.	12 mm
1 in.	2.5 cm

Liquid Measurements

USA	METRIC	UK
2 tbsp.	30 ml	1 fl. oz.
¼ cup	60 ml	2 fl. oz.
⅓ cup	80 ml	3 fl. oz.
½ cup	125 ml	4 fl. oz.
⅔ cup	160 ml	5 fl. oz.
¾ cup	180 ml	6 fl. oz.
1 cup	250 ml	8 fl. oz.
1½ cups	375 ml	12 fl. oz.
2 cups	500 ml	16 fl. oz.

Abbreviations

USA/UK	Metric
oz = ounce	g = gram
lb = pound	kg = kilogram
in = inch	mm = millimeter
ft = foot	cm = centimeter
tbsp = tablespoon	ml = milliliter
teaspoon = teaspoon	l = liter
fl oz = fluid ounce	
qt = quart	

Retail Accessories List

Baking Accessories

	Description	Brand Name	Size	Usage	Qty Fit in Ninja
	White porcelain. Oven to table serving. Good for souffles, personal-size quiches, desserts, and individual servings of sides.	BIA Blanc De Table	5" round	Quiches, souffles, sides, dips	2
	White porcelain. Oven to table serving. Good for souffles, personal size quiches, desserts, and individual servings of sides.	BIA Blanc De Table	6" oval	Crème brûlée	2
	Ramekins – white porcelain. Oven to table.	HIC	6 ounce each – 3½" round	Souffles	4
	Individual mini cupcake pans – metal	Foxrun	3¼" round	Cupcakes	4
	Individual mini cupcake pans – metal	Foxrun	2¼" round	Mini cupcakes	8
	Cake pops – fast and easy way to make cake pops. Includes food-grade nonstick silicone 2-piece tray, 50 sticks, and decorating guide. Use with any cake mix.	As seen on TV – TastyTop	8" x 5"	Cake pops	1 tray makes 8 pops
	Create a giant cupcake that the whole party can enjoy! Comes with 2-piece silicone cake pan and filling insert. Filling ideas – ice cream, pudding, gelatin, fruit, candy, or whip cream.	As seen on TV – Big Top Cupcake	7½" x 4" round	Giant cupcake	1
	Petite stoneware dish for personal-size desserts and quiches. Multicolor.	Le Creuset	4¼"	Tarts, flans, quiches, meals	2
	Nonstick petite tart pan	Wilton	4" x ¾" round	Tarts, quiches	2
	6 oz. custard glass cups	Anchor	3¾" x 2" round	Custards, mini cakes, reheating food	3

Retail Accessories List

	Description	Brand Name	Size	Usage	Qty Fit in Ninja
	Baking Accessories				
	Mini pie baking kit	Nordicware	7" round	Pies, potpies, quiches, tarts	1
	6" round cake pan - nonstick	WS - Goldtouch Nonstick	6" round	Cakes	1
	4" round cake pan - nonstick	WS - Goldtouch Nonstick	4" round	Individual-size cakes	2
	2" timbale molds	William Sonoma	2" pans	Petite souffles, brioches, french cakes, or popovers	6
	Silicone baking cups	Regency Silicups	4" round	Cupcakes, candy, muffins, quiches	6
	Silicone mini baking cups	Regency Silicups	2" round	Mini cupcakes, candy, muffins, quiches	12
	Disposable foil mini loaf pan	Durable Foil	5⅝" x 3⁹/₁₆" x 1¹⁵/₁₆"	Mini breads, cakes	2
	Disposable foil loaf pan	Durable Foil	8" x 3¾" x 2⅜"	Breads, cakes, meatloaf	1
	Heart-shaped mini cake pans	Chloe Kitchen	3" x 3¼"	Mini cakes	4
	4" tube pans	Chloe Kitchen	4" round	Mini cakes	2
	Mini loaf pan - nonstick	Chloe Kitchen	5½" x 2¾"	Mini breads and meatloaf	2

Retail Accessories List

Roasting Accessories				
Description	**Brand Name**	**Size**	**Usage**	**Qty Fit in Ninja**
Oval au gratin dish – porcelain. Oven to table.	Apilco	10" x 5½" x 1⅓"	Casseroles	1
Disposable foil rectangle pan	Mainstays	6" x 8" x 2½"	Casseroles, roasts, chicken, fish	1
Disposable foil rectangle pan	Mainstays	7.37" x 5¼" x 1¾" H	Casseroles, roasts, chicken, fish	1
Disposable foil pan	Hefty	8" x 4"	Meatloaf	1
1.5 qt. round side dish	CorningWare	7½" x 2½" round	Casseroles, roasts, chicken, fish	1
Oval mini casserole dishes. Ceramic. Oven to table	CorningWare	5½" H x 3" x 2½"	Mini casseroles, sides, onion soup	2
Pouch pods. Silicone form. Floats in water during cooking.	Fusion Brands	3½" x 2½"	Poached eggs, frittatas, baked goods	5
Flexible grilling skewers	FireWire	24"	Meat, seafood, vegetable skewers	1
Spice bags	Regency	4" x 3"	Flavor meats, chicken, fish, and vegetables	1

Retail Accessories List

	Description	Brand Name	Size	Usage	Qty Fit in Ninja
Roasting Accessories					
	Flavor injector	BBB Exclusive	N/A	Meat and poultry	1
	Porcelain baking dishes	Home Essentials & Beyond	5" x 5" square	Mini casseroles, hot dips, reheat	1
	Meat thermometer	Polder	N/A	Meat and poultry	1

139

Recipes by Cooking Function

 STEAM-INFUSED ROASTING

 FAST ONE-POT MEAL MAKING

 SEARious SLOW COOKING

Recipes by Cooking Function

 STEAM-INFUSED BAKING

 STOVETOP OR OVEN COOKING

Index

Index